SR-71

Inside Lockheed's
BLACKBIRD

Text by Michael O'Leary
Photography by Eric Schulzinger and Michael O'Leary

Motorbooks International
Publishers & Wholesalers

First published in 1991 by Motorbooks International Publishers & Wholesalers, PO Box 2, 729 Prospect Avenue, Osceola, WI 54020 USA

Motorbooks International books are also available at discounts in bulk quantity for industrial or sales-promotional use. For details write to Special Sales Manager at the Publisher's address

Library of Congress Cataloging-in-Publication Data
O'Leary, Michael (Michael D.)
    SR-71 / Michael O'Leary and Eric
      Schulzinger. p.   cm.
    Includes bibliographical references and
      index.
    ISBN 0-87938-541-3
    1. SR-71 (Jet reconnaissance plane)
    I. Schulzinger, Eric. II. Title.
UG1242.R40437 1991
358.4'583—dc20   91-3066

Printed and bound in Hong Kong

On the front cover: *A Blackbird soars upward in a high-angle pullup.*

On the back cover: Top, *a Blackbird greedily gulps fuel from a KC–135;* bottom left, *pilot Dan House and RSO Blair Bozek look up from their Blackbird's cockpit;* bottom right, *the SR-71 maintenance personnel pose with the last of the Blackbirds.*

On the frontispiece: *Although the Blackbird fleet was decimated by what, in the authors' opinion, was a premature (especially in light of the Gulf War) retirement, the future is not completely bleak since three aircraft have been assigned to NASA to help develop advanced concepts for a new generation of aircraft like the X-30 "national space plane."*

On the title page: *Thumbs up—these guys were great! The maintenance personnel responsible for the moving and positioning of the Blackbird group portrait at Beale AFB.*

On the acknowledgments page: *Streaming fuel, an SR-71A makes a break for landing over Beale Air Force Base.*

Contents

Acknowledgments

To create a book like this requires the positive assistance of a great many people. First, we would like to thank all the men and women of the US Air Force and 9th Strategic Reconnaissance Wing who supported the Blackbird through many adversities. We would also like to offer special thanks to Ben Rich, Fred Carmody, Rich Stadler, the men and women of Lockheed's Skunk Works, Tom Clancy, Terry Pappas, Chuck Guizzo, Gary Hultquist, Brent Thompson, Norb Budzinski, Andy Stumpf, Assistant DCM Bill Morton, chiefs Davis and Applehof, MSgt. Steve Koren, NASA/Dryden Public Affairs Office (especially Don Hailey and Nancy Lovato), Steve Ishmael, Rogers Smith, Bob Meyer and Marta Bohn-Meyer.

Special thanks for the love and support from Jeri, David, Matthew, Lynn and Bad Buster who liked *all* the Blackbirds.

Foreword

They're gone now. Just a few months ago I saw two of them in a museum, still looking like something from a science-fiction movie, hulking, ominous shapes of slate black.

They come from another era, one in which the government could go to a master designer and say, "We need a special airplane. Can you build it?" Designed, built, and tested in a brief flicker of time, the SR-71 was and is the class of the world, even sitting still. So much about the Blackbird is still secret—like how fast it can really go (probably something like 2,400 miles per hour—maybe a little more), all the places they went, and all the things they did. And all the missiles that burned out trying to catch them.

The Blackbird is testimony to a simple fact: national defense is less about killing people than it is about finding things out. War and peace are about having the right information at the right time. If you know what you need to know, you can take the necessary action to forestall a conflict; and if there is a war underway, you can use good information to maximize harm to the enemy while minimizing harm to your own people.

The SR-71s never shot anything more lethal than film, but the importance of the information they gathered can be understood by the aircraft itself. No aircraft ever made needed the speed and altitude capabilities of this bird. The SR-71 was one of the first stealth aircraft, certainly the first to use RAM (radar-absorbing material) in its leading edges. It was made to go in harm's way, and following John Paul Jones' axiom, it wasn't designed to go there slowly. Approaching at what pilots call the speed of heat, it would give scant warning to alert defenders, and after they learned of its passage—the sonic boom is not especially stealthy—it was too late. Catching something going over 3,000 feet per second (the speed of a .300 Winchester Magnum bullet) is very nearly impossible. Not bad for 1950s technology. If there is a replacement for this aircraft, at this writing it's even blacker than the SR-71's airframe. Though there are rumors . . . .

The fact of the matter is that the Blackbird was retired before its time. There is as yet nothing to take its place. Satellites take fine pictures, but they are regulated by immutable laws of physics. A satellite cannot overfly any place more than twice a day, and those appointments in time and space are easily predicted. Worse, they cannot be tailored to avoid cloud cover, cannot be arranged to surprise the people whose activities interest us. Satellites, while supremely useful and, in their way, reliable, are inflexible, and flexibility is the heart of national security. With the Blackbird, a commander could turn to his intelligence officer and say, "I need information on this spot, and I need it *fast!*" That information could then be had in a matter of hours. No longer.

In January of this year we sent our people to war without hour-to-hour reconnaissance capability. Some American troops went "over the berm" into Kuwait and Iraq without timely information concerning what was on the other side. Remarkably, our people didn't suffer for it. That was more luck than design, and while luck is useful, it is not dependable. Since there was no price to pay, those who made this incorrect decision will be able to say that the capability was not all that necessary after all. The field commanders who wanted that information have already said otherwise, but some decisions, however wrong they may have been, cannot be reversed. The Blackbird is gone, almost certainly for good, a decoration for museums, a monument to Kelly Johnson, Ben Rich, and a number of other engineering geniuses. That it could have kept going is tribute to the aircraft and its builders; that it did its job so well for nearly thirty years is testimony to the way things used to be—and still could be if we remembered how to do things right instead of the bureaucratic way.

—*Tom Clancy*

Kelly's Magnificent Machine

On 22 December 1964, aviation history was made when Lockheed test pilot Robert J. Gilliland lifted off from Palmdale, California, in the prototype SR-71A, USAF s/n 64-17950,—the aircraft that would later become world famous as the "Blackbird." To understand how and why the creation of this fabulous machine came about, it is necessary to go back into the 1950s and examine the SR-71's predecessors.

The Lockheed U-2 spyplane had been developed under great secrecy by Kelly Johnson's Skunk Works during the early 1950s to meet a Central Intelligence Agency (CIA) requirement for a high-flying intelligence-gathering platform that would be impervious to the Soviet Union's interceptor fleet and force of primitive surface-to-air missiles (SAMs). Operated out of bases in Turkey, Japan, and Britain, the U-2 was highly successful in its mission. The Soviets knew the aircraft was overflying their industrial and military facilities, but there was little they could do about it. Numerous interceptions were attempted and hundreds of SAMs were blasted at the all-black U-2s as they slowly traversed what was previously forbidden territory, gathering massive quantities of information for CIA specialists.

On 1 May 1960, the CIA's dream spying situation ceased to exist when a U-2 (variously identified as USAF s/n 56-6693, NASA 360, and CIA Article

The seed for the Blackbird was sown in a proposal created by Kelly Johnson and Ben Rich called the CL-400—a massive hydrogen fueled aircraft of advanced design that would promise not only high speed but also good unrefueled range.

361) was knocked down near Sverdlovsk. There is still some doubt on how the U-2 was actually downed, but the Soviets recently commented that the U-2 was blasted from the sky by a barrage of SA-2 SAMs, which also accidentally destroyed a MiG interceptor that was trying to get the U-2. It is thought that a direct hit was not made on the U-2 but that shrapnel from a nearby burst did enough damage to the fragile U-2 that the airframe started to come apart. Francis Gary Powers, the pilot, floated down by parachute to Mother Russia to become a prisoner and an instant international figure.

U-2 operations were cut back and overflights of the Soviet Union ceased. However, this did not mean that the U-2's career had come to an end—far from it.

Clarence L. "Kelly" Johnson began his career with Lockheed in 1933. Born in Ishpeming, Michigan, on 27 February 1910, Kelly learned about tools and mechanical construction from his father—a Swedish immigrant who was a carpenter and bricklayer.

By the age of twelve, young Johnson was already fascinated by the newly emerging science of aeronautics and knew that his future was in the air. Kelly went on to study aeronautical engineering at the University of Michigan and, while studying for his master's degree, helped improve the aerodynamics of Indianapolis 500 racing cars.

Being hired by Lockheed was a major step for the engineer since the company gave him a base from which to develop his innovative ideas. Within four years, at the age of twenty-seven, Kelly was awarded the Lawrence Sperry Award for outstanding

aeronautical achievement for his work with Lockheed's family of high-speed twin-engine transports.

The Skunk Works was created in 1943 to develop America's first operational jet fighter—the P-80 Shooting Star. The Skunk Works took its name from a foul-smelling moonshine distillery in Al Capp's then-popular comic strip *Li'l Abner*. Johnson believed that a small group of talented individuals operating under great secrecy and relatively free from company and government red tape could do great things quickly. He was right.

The Skunk Works rapidly became an institution at Lockheed and, after the successful development of the Shooting Star, went on to create fabulous aircraft like the double-Mach F-104 Starfighter. During this time, Johnson also kept his hand in on other more conventional aircraft like the Lockheed Constellation and Neptune. In 1954, the Skunk Works became an autonomous unit of Lockheed, complete with its own manufacturing facilities. The complex was given the formal name of Advanced Development Projects (ADP). At this time, ADP's most pressing project was bidding for a contract that would eventually result in the U-2. By using Johnson's commonsense rules of business and aeronautical construction, Lockheed was able to beat out all other competitors with ADP's offer to build twenty U-2 spyplanes for a total of $22,000,000 and deliver these aircraft to the CIA in an amazing eight-month time period.

Knowing that the U-2 would eventually be vulnerable to growing Soviet air defenses (the CIA estimated that U-2s could be successfully operated over the Soviet Union for three years before the first shoot down would occur), the CIA began searching for proposals for a more advanced platform that would be invulnerable to an advanced air defense system.

In 1956, the Skunk Works began to look at more advanced planes. In order to simplify the work process, the first step was to gauge just how much growth was left in the basic U-2 airframe. Modifications were considered to increase altitude and performance. "We made many studies and tests to improve the survivability of the U-2 by attempting to fly higher and faster as well as reducing its radar cross section and providing both infrared and radar jamming gear," recalled Johnson. However, the team concluded that it was probably best to wipe the slate clean and come up with an entirely new design.

In order to counter Soviet defenses and accomplish the intelligence gathering mission in the quickest possible order, a top speed of over Mach 3 was a requirement (and this speed would have to be held for a lengthy period of time). Also, the plane would have to operate at over 80,000 feet and incorporate advanced design principles to reduce its radar signature (three decades later, this technique would pick up the popular term "stealth"). For safety of operations, two engines would be required. Knowing that the new craft's speed and altitude would not protect it forever, the CIA also specified that a suite of electronic countermeasures (ECM) be added to the design. The design would have to encompass adequate room for carrying a variety of sensors and have the ability to conform to changes of sensor packages.

The task was daunting because the new plane would be operating in an unknown and very hostile atmosphere—an atmosphere alien to

SR-71A noses are interchangeable for varying missions that may call for specialized sensor packs. Crew chiefs and other ground crew members often decorated various portions of the Blackbird (usually the vertical tails) with art work drawn with chalk. This highly decorated nose is seen mounted on its transportation dolly.

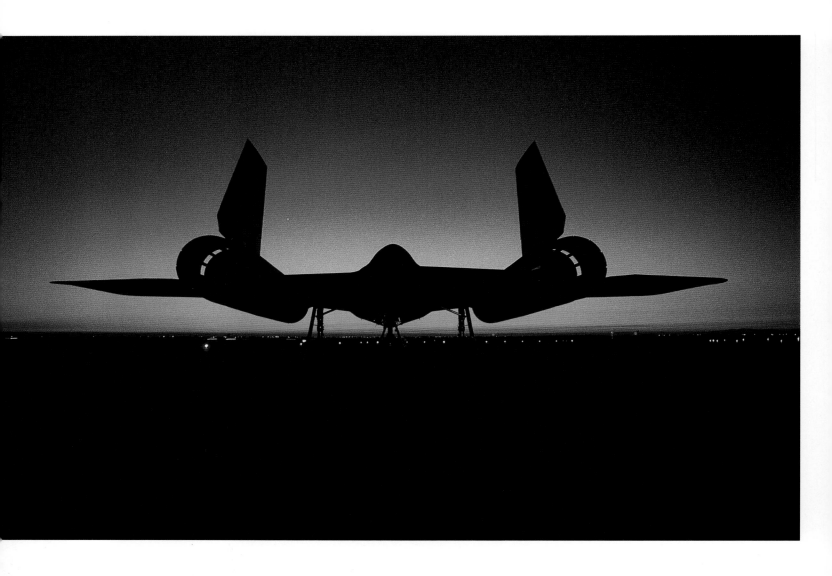

the human body, aircraft fluids and the majority of metals and other elements used in aircraft construction.

Competition was intense from other companies who also wanted to obtain the lucrative contract. "We were evaluated against some very interesting designs by General Dynamics and a Navy design," recalled Johnson in the late 1970s. "This latter concept was proposed as a ramjet-powered rubber inflatable machine,

initially carried to altitude by a balloon and then rocket boosted to a speed where the ramjets could produce thrust. Our studies on this aircraft proved it to be totally infeasible. The carrying balloon had to be a mile in diameter to lift the unit, which had a proposed wing area of 1/7th of an acre!"

With increasing speed, the skin of an aircraft begins to heat as it passes through the atmosphere. This is caused by an advancing flow of molecules passing over the airframe. As speed increases, the flow of molecules increases and the heat factor rapidly begins to build. Aluminum, the most common metal used in aircraft construction, is a "soft" metal that does not hold up to high skin temperatures that are encountered in Mach 3 flight. In order to meet and defeat the heat problem, the new design would have to

be built of titanium and stainless steel alloys. Other new materials would have to be developed including new plastics, fluids for the aircraft's systems, and wiring that would not distort and come apart. Even the tires would have to be built out of a new material since regular rubber would begin to burn at the temperatures caused by the speed that the new plane would attain.

Lockheed had begun working with titanium as early as 1949. A difficult metal at best, much study and development had to be undertaken to determine how it could be used in aircraft construction. Assisted by the talented Ben Rich, Johnson worked to overcome the many complex problems caused by the high requirements. "We attempted to attain high strength-weight ratios, good ductility, and relatively cheap structures, which did not develop very rapidly," Johnson stated. "There were no control cables which would take the required number of cycles safely. We had to have special ones made of Elgiloy, the material used for watch springs."

Much of the equipment for the new design would have to be specially manufactured by vendors since the complexity of the project meant that the complete aircraft could not be constructed by the small Skunk Works team. "In the field of equipment there was an amazing lack of high temperature electronic gear, particularly in the areas of wires, plugs, transducers and so on. Many vendors told us they had transducers good for 1000 degrees Farenheit operating temperatures, but when we tested the gear we found it had mainly been designed for rocket testing and its life span was very short. Due essentially to temperature lag, the inside of the unit seldom got hot. There were no hydraulic fluids or pumps that could take operating temperatures continuously of approximately 600 degrees Farenheit. There were no hydraulic seals suitable for such an environment," said Johnson.

The A-12 (a Lockheed designation) handily won the contract since the other entrants were basically unworkable. The contract was awarded on 29 August 1959 and the CIA specified that scale models be tested and a full-scale mockup be constructed. On 30 January 1960, the final contract came through for the completion of design work, manufacturing and testing of a dozen A-12s.

As related elsewhere in this volume, the construction of a suitable powerplant was an absolute must, and Pratt & Whitney did a magnificent job

Next page
A low sun lights up the black "iron ball" paint finish on the SR-71A. Note the temporary art work, the logo for Dolby Noise Reduction, on the vertical tail.

With the withdrawal of the Blackbird fleet from active duty, the skies over Beale will never again witness blistering passes and high-angle pullups as the SRs returned from missions or training flights.

in creating the J58 bypass turbojet engine which developed 32,500 pounds of static thrust in afterburner at sea level. When operating at over Mach 3, fuel consumption is approximately 8,000 gallons of JP-7 (a special-formula, very high altitude jet fuel) per hour.

The first set of J58s was not ready for the prototype A-12 due to some developmental problems. Constructed under great secrecy at Burbank, portions of the A-12 were moved to the secret test facility at Groom Lake, Nevada. At this location, the plane was assembled and readied for test flights. Two J75s were substituted for the J58s and, although a reliable powerplant, the engines produced much less thrust.

First flight occurred on 26 April 1962 as pilot Lou Schalk took the single-seat aircraft aloft and into the unknown. With the substitute engines, the A-12 could just edge past Mach 1 so full airframe and systems testing could not be undertaken. However, the J58s were installed in the first part of 1963 and the A-12 was ready for Mach 3.

On 29 February 1964, President Lyndon B. Johnson revealed to the American public the existence of a new, highly advanced aircraft that appeared as if it had come from an alien world. Using photographs of the new plane to illustrate his point, Johnson referred to the plane as an A-11 rather than as an A-12. Also, the photographs were of another variant—the YF-12A prototype interceptor. The aeronautical press was stunned since secrecy involving the new aircraft had been very, very good. President Johnson never got down to stating what the new aircraft's role was or who was operating the plane.

By early 1964 the CIA was operating the A-12 around the world on classified missions and several of the aircraft were lost in training and operational accidents. One of the most curious of the A-12 modifications was the mounting of a pylon atop the rear fuselage to carry a single D-21 ramjet

The USAF confirmed that SR-71As had been fired on over 1,000 times by hostile missiles during its operational career. Due to the immense speed, altitude, and stealth capabilities of the Blackbird, a hit was never achieved.

reconnaissance drone that could be launched into heavily defended targets to gather information. However, the A-12 and D-12 were both destroyed during the first test separation, resulting in one fatality. From that point on, the D-21s were tested under the wings of a modified B-52. The A-12 fleet was withdrawn from use around 1968 and put into storage at Lockheed's Plant 42 at Palmdale, California.

The USAF had been observing the development of the A-12 with great interest and felt there was potential for making the aircraft into an interceptor to destroy a perceived threat from a new generation of Soviet manned bombers.

The YF-12A, as the interceptor was designated, would mount the advanced Hughes ASG-18/GAR-19 fire control and missile system and have a two-man crew. A large folding fin was added under the rear fuselage to help increase stability and this unit was folded flat during takeoff and landing. Built-in missile bays carried three new AIM-47A missiles.

The YF-12As were assembled at Groom Lake and the first plane flew on 7 August 1963 with James Eastham at the controls. Only three YF-12As were built but the planes helped increase the USAF's knowledge of high-speed flight and more modern weapons systems. Launching a missile at Mach 3 was, in itself, a major problem. Kelly Johnson commented, "Great difficulty existed in obtaining instrumentation satisfactory for measuring pressures and air velocity over the speed altitude spectrum. This is particularly true of conditions in the engine inlet and ejector. This necessitated the development of water-cooled instrumentation packages, which were quite clumsy, but did provide a means for making the millions of pressure

In a direct response to the threat imposed by the Blackbird upon their military/industrial establishment, the Soviets developed the MiG-25. When Lt. Viktor Belenko defected to Japan with his MiG-25 on 6 September 1976, he confirmed that the new MiGs had been used operationally on Blackbird intercepts but could not get their intended targets.

measurements required through the development tests.

"I would say the greatest problem encountered in-flight had to do with the transonic speed region, where it was extremely difficult to correlate the results from wind tunnel tests and flight tests.

"The next greatest problem had to do with the development of the air inlet control system, which involved scheduling the air inlet spike position, and various by-pass door arrangements, to maintain the optimum shock position on the cowl, and minimum drag. Operating forces as high as fourteen tons can develop on the spike. This requires massive hydraulic power and extremely fast sensing of the various design parameters to restart the inlet.

"The aircraft showed itself to have excellent flight characteristics throughout its speed range, particularly on takeoff and landing. Visibility was good, but the pilots initially complained of a very high glare flying at high altitudes. The use of non-reflective coatings on instruments, and other areas, definitely helped this condition."

Hughes had developed an excellent weapon system (forerunner of today's efficient and combat-tested Phoenix) in the pulse-Doppler ASG-18 radar unit and GAR-9 (later redesignated AIM-74A) long-range missile. These systems had originally been developed for the North American F-108 Rapier, an advanced stainless-steel interceptor, but when that program had been cancelled because of technical delays and cost overruns, the missile and radar were transferred to the Lockheed project.

The second cockpit in the YF-12A was occupied by the Fire Control Officer (FCO) who operated the radar to acquire, track and fire at hostile targets. Because of the high speed of the YF-12A, a missile launch could travel up to 150 miles and the tracking system was sophisticated enough to

A Blackbird departs Beale. Even the cows grazing in the farmland surrounding the base had become accustomed to the white heat explosions as the J58s hurtled the Blackbird aloft on its mission.

A sight never seen before: The doors to all the sheds housing the operational Blackbirds at Beale are opened at once during January 1990 especially for this book.

track and destroy supersonic targets at altitudes between sea level and 100,000 feet. After three years of testing and fine tuning, the system was enjoying a ninety percent success rate against drone targets.

A definitive F-12B interceptor for the USAF was cancelled by the Kennedy Administration's new secretary of defense, Robert Strange McNamara, who wanted aircraft that could operate in multi-role missions. Thus, the General Dynamics F-111 was born even though Congress had

initially voted a large budget for the development of the F-12B. Two YF-12As were passed on to NASA for high-speed research concerning commercial transports while the third machine became the SR-71C.

On 24 July 1964, President Johnson once again stunned the aviation world when he revealed the existence of a new Lockheed plane, the SR-71A—an aircraft dedicated to strategic reconnaissance with performance so advanced that no other aircraft (Allied or Soviet) could catch the machine. President Johnson made a slight error in his speech (once again), referring to the new design as SR-71 rather than the correct RS-71 and the new designation stuck.

During January 1961, Kelly Johnson and his team made a first

proposal for an advanced strategic reconnaissance aircraft to government officials. The meeting was favorable and ADP began to make initial studies into what would become the SR-71A. Opposition came from certain USAF officers who favored the massive North American XB-70 program, which had run into some problems as a bomber and was not being considered as a strategic reconnaissance platform.

An SR-71A mockup was built and the USAF liked what they saw. Johnson continued discussions with Gen. Curtis LeMay, commander of Strategic Air Command (SAC) and, on 28 December 1962, a contract was issued for the production of six SR-71As. Johnson recalled the basic design features of the plane, along with the aircraft's mission requirements, "Having chosen the

A Blackbird in its shed. Today, the sheds stand empty at Beale and it is not known if they will be torn down or utilized for another purpose.

required performance in speed, altitude, and range, it was immediately evident that a thin delta-wing platform was required with a very moderate wing loading to allow flight at very high altitude. A long, slender fuselage was necessary to contain most of the fuel as well as the landing gear and payloads. To reduce the wing trim drag, the fuselage was fitted with lateral surfaces called chines, which actually converted the forward fuselage into a fixed canard which developed lift.

"The hardest design problem on the airplane was making the engine air inlet and ejector work properly. The inlet cone moves almost three feet to keep the shock wave where we want it. A hydraulic actuator, computer controlled, has to provide operating forces of up to 31,000 pounds under certain flow conditions in the nacelles. To account for the effect of the fuselage chine airflow, the inlets are pointed down and in toward the fuselage.

"The use of dual vertical tails canted inward on the engine nacelles took advantage of the chine vortex in such a way that the directional stability improves as the angle of attack of the aircraft increases."

To the casual observer, the A-12, YF-12A and SR-71A look like the same aircraft. Yet, there are many important differences between them—both in mission and design. For example, the gross weight of the SR-71 is about 172,000 pounds, compared to the 120,000-pound gross weight of the A-12. The SR-71 is longer and has broader chines while the second cockpit houses the Reconnaissance Systems Officer (RSO).

Test flying on the first SR-71A was well underway during 1965, and the program was soon joined by the next two planes from the production line. Much was learned about operating such a high-performance recon platform. Two aircraft experienced tire blowout on landing, resulting in the planes leaving the runway and catching fire. Modifications to the tires and wheels corrected this fault.

In 1965, the 4200th Strategic Reconnaissance Wing (SRW) was activated at Beale AFB with the SR-71 and Beale remained the type's main base until its retirement. The 4200th

Three of Lockheed's unique designs are seen at Beale on 11 October 1990. In the foreground is a TR-1A Dragon Lady, in the middle is an F-117A Stealth Fighter, while in the background is Beale's new static display SR-71A mounted on a special concrete base shaped like the distinctive Mach 3 insignia worn by Blackbird crews.

was redesignated as the 9th SRW just 1½ years later. In a consolidation of resources, the 9th SRW absorbed the Lockheed U-2s of the 99th Strategic Reconnaissance Squadron (SRS), thus making Beale the major US strategic reconnaissance base.

Overseas deployment of the SR fleet started early on—especially since the Vietnam War was heating up and intelligence was critical. To cover Vietnam, the 9th SRW opened up Detachment 1 at Kadena, Okinawa, and intensive operations began in 1968. Detachment 4 opened at RAF Mildenhall, England, during 1967 and usually fielded two SR-71As. These two detachments (or Dets) proved to be the most active of all the Dets and forward operating locations (FOL).

Although outside the scope of this book, descriptions of the missions undertaken by the SR-71 would fill volumes. In fact, the government was going to declassify the majority of

SR-71 mission data in October 1991 but, at the last minute—and for unknown reasons—this has been delayed.

This book takes an overall look at the Blackbird and its last year of operations before its premature retirement. Certainly the Blackbird retired as a champion and as one of the most decorated of all USAF aircraft.

Kelly Johnson went on to collect many awards in recognition of his aeronautical achievements. Included in these laurels: the Collier Trophy, the Theodore Von Karman Award, the Thomas D. White National Defense Award, the National Medal of Science, the Sylvanus Albert Reed Award from the American Institute of Aeronautics

A TR-1B dual control trainer. With the Blackbirds gone, the Dragon Ladies now form the "black" contingent at the base.

and Astronautics (twice), the Kitty Hawk Memorial Award, and the National Security Medal from Ronald Reagan. In 1974, Kelly was inducted into the Aviation Hall of Fame.

Johnson retired from Lockheed in 1975 with the title of senior vice president and left the company's board of directors in 1980. In 1987, Lockheed donated $350,000 to Caltech to establish the Clarence L. Johnson Professorship in Aeronautics.

On 21 December 1990, Kelly Johnson passed away from medical complications in a Burbank hospital. Like the SR-71, he went out a winner.

The Need for Speed

How do you create an engine with the performance and reliability required for an aircraft with the performance parameters of the Lockheed SR-71? The answer: With a great deal of secrecy and Yankee ingenuity! Studies for the powerplant that would eventually emerge as the Pratt & Whitney J58 began in 1955, only ten years after the conclusion of World War II. Oddly, it was the US Navy that instigated the project; they wanted an engine that would be capable of supplying an aircraft with Mach 3 dash capability. The project was cloaked in secrecy and only a small cadre of specialized engineers and technicians worked on the powerplant.

The prototype engine was run for the first time on Christmas Eve of 1957, giving an idea of just how much had been accomplished in a short period of time. At this point, the Navy's interest began to wane but Lockheed, the USAF and the CIA had plans for the groundwork undertaken by Pratt & Whitney (P&W). The J58 program evolved to meet the requirements for an engine to operate continuously at more than Mach 3 and go higher than 80,000 feet.

Later, a unique design feature of the J58 was added: A bleed bypass system that consisted of three large diameter pipes running along each side

SR-71 engine start is a very noisy procedure and all crewmen wear protective ear coverings. The roar from the self-start system (located within each Blackbird protective hangar at Beale) and the engine start itself provide an ear-damaging racket. Note the JP-7 leaking from the fueled Blackbird, the leaking will not stop until the SR-71 reaches cruise speed and altitude.

of the engine. At high Mach, a portion of the air would bypass the compressor and turbine sections, giving the engine stallfree operation. The bleed bypass feature led to the popular description of the J58 as being a turbo-ramjet. Obviously, the J58 and SR-71 were made for each other.

Prototype J58 engines were flown as early as 1962, and the first production engines, known as YJs, flew a short time later. The only major modification to the engine design occurred in 1964 when a lightweight afterburner and a variable vane inlet case were incorporated, make a K variant of the powerplant. Continuous operation in military and afterburner conditions were also unique to this engine's design requirements. Currently, the J58 is unique in that it is the only engine rated for continuous afterburning.

The J58 can operate continuously at more than Mach 3. Temperatures generated by this speed required that engine parts be made of high temperature alloys. Titanium placed in the very front of the engine was chosen for weight considerations, while Waspaloy, a nickel-iron alloy, was chosen for most other components. Other alloys used include Inconel, Astroloy, Hastelloy-X and Haynes-25.

The control system of the J58 is purely hydromechanical, again because of temperature considerations in the nacelle. A remotely located, closed-loop feedback electronic control is used for in-flight trimming of the engine.

Fuel is not only used for combustion, but as the hydraulic fluid, and as the primary coolant of all control system components. Even the engine oil is unique because it is pure synthetic, polyphenyl ether and

A huge J58 afterburner can. With afterburners in operation, the J58s can pump out 32,500 pounds of thrust each—consuming 8,000 gallons of JP-7 per hour in the process.

Surrounded by an ocean of heat waves, an SR-71A's right Pratt & Whitney J58 comes to life with a squirt of TEB (tetraethyl borane). Since the JP-7 fuel has such a high flash point, the TEB is injected directly into the engine at start to lower ignition point and allow for starting and producing the unearthly green glow that characterizes SR starts.

chemically stable up to 650 degrees Fahrenheit.

"The J58 is the best engine in the world," states Lockheed's Ben Rich. "The first flight of the A-12 took place on 26 April 1962 and we've never had a stall at cruise speed. Can you imagine that? Nearly 28 years and we've never had an engine stall."

Development responsibility of the J58 was assigned to P&W's William Brown (now retired). "In the early days of the J58 program," recalls Brown, "it was so secret only a half dozen people in East Hartford [Pratt & Whitney headquarters] were in on it. I'd go to Washington, go to a street corner, get into a car and go to another corner, get into another car and perhaps go to certain inconspicuous buildings for our conferences. It was the same way going out to Lockheed."

The Pratt & Whitney J58 stands out as a major American aeronautical achievement—a powerplant that was built on schedule and for a reasonable cost to fulfill a requirement many people thought impossible. Fortunately, the J58's mighty roar has not been completely stilled with the retirement of the USAF's SR-71 fleet. The Blackbirds operated by NASA will soon begin operations—once more filling the empty desert skies with the awesome roar of American technology at its best.

The powerplant that Ben Rich calls the best engine in the world. The Pratt & Whitney J58 was truly an amazing engine for its day. This detailed display example illustrates the bleed bypass system that consists of three large diameter pipes running along each side of the engine. The silver object on the forward top portion of the powerplant is the TEB tank.

With both J58s running smoothly and all hangar checks successfully completed, an SR-71A prepares to depart its Beale hangar. In order to gain momentum, the pilot briefly advances the throttles to get the plane out of the hangar and then brings them back a bit for taxi to the active.

Before the advent of the built-in self-start systems in each Beale AFB Blackbird protective hangar, J58 starting was achieved with these custom-made carts powered by hot-rodded auto engines. This start cart is seen on the Beale ramp during February 1990.

Once in the runup area, the crew would assure that all systems were fully operational, including the J58s, before launching on the mission. Even with the extremely high demands placed on the J58, it is one of the most successful aircraft engines ever built.

The drama that was Beale. In the closing days of SR-71A operations, a Blackbird lifts off for a crew check flight. The J58s are seen producing their characteristic diamond shock pattern. On takeoff, a further squirt of TEB was needed to get the burners going.

Next page
In the cold, remote, and hostile edges of near outer space, the Pratt & Whitney J58s have operated admirably for the SR-71 fleet for nearly thirty years.

Blackbird crew R-12: Maj. Terry Pappas (left) and Maj. John Manzi pose with their favorite aircraft. Both men wear the bulky 50-pound Dave Clark S1030 high-altitude suits that cost $120,000 each.

Flying the Blackbird

by Terry Pappas

Terry Pappas, major, USAF, was an SR-71 aircraft commander, squadron assistant operations officer and T-38 instructor pilot and flight examiner for the 9th Strategic Reconnaissance Wing, Beale AFB, California. He is a command pilot with over 5,000 hours flying time in the SR-71, B-52, T-38 and numerous civilian aircraft. Pappas is currently a T-38 instructor pilot in support of the Air Force Flight Test Center operations at Edwards AFB, California. The other member of this two-man crew was John Manzi, major, USAF, an SR-71 reconnaissance systems officer (RSO). He is a senior navigator with over 2,000 hours of flying time in the SR-71, F-111 and RF-4. Manzi is currently attending the Armed Forces Intermediate Service School. Pappas and Manzi were selected as Strategic Air Command's (SAC) Reconnaissance Crew of the Year for 1987 and SAC's nominee for the Air Force Association's General O'Malley Award for 1988.

How fast does an SR-71 really fly? The public's curiosity about one of the world's most intriguing aircraft, the SR-71 Blackbird, seems endless. There are straightforward queries: At 80,000 feet, what is the view? How do pilots eat and drink while trapped in that space suit? There are, as well, more politically sensitive pursuits: What countries have you overflown? Have you been shot at while flying the Blackbird? What in-flight emergencies have you had? As an SR-71 Aircraft Commander with over 5,000 hours flying time and twenty years of experience, I will explore these and many other questions concerning this amazing and intriguing machine.

Flying the Blackbird is exhilarating and exhausting. Takeoff is a bit violent as each engine's afterburner ignites, rarely at the same instant, jerking the aircraft hard to one side then the other. There's nothing quite like releasing the brakes and pushing both throttles slowly to full military power, then into minimum afterburner. Once both afterburners are successfully lit, it's time to push both throttles to full burner. The aircraft rumbles a little at first, resisting the tremendous forces placed on it by the big jet engines, then the Blackbird surrenders and it's one smooth ever-increasing rate of acceleration. What a ride! Things begin happening so fast, and a momentary distraction can cause everything to become a blur.

Part of the intrigue of flying the SR-71 is the level of concentration required to tame this beast. Within seconds of brake release, it's time to pull back on the stick at 180 knots indicated airspeed. No sooner is the nose up than it is off the ground at 210 knots. The gear must be retracted immediately to preclude exceeding the gear limit speed. Pulling the nose higher as we rapidly approach 400 knots in the climb, my navigator (Reconnaissance Systems Officer—RSO) and I exchange a few quick cockpit checks and I settle in to just hanging on to this beautiful black animal of incredible power and aggressively clear the flight path, glancing back inside the cockpit frequently to confirm that precise parameters are being met.

The vertical velocity indicator is pegged at maximum and the altimeter is spinning like a top as we race upward. Lateral pressure on the stick is required as we roll into a turn to intercept the outbound course while carefully checking bank angle, pitch attitude, indicated airspeed, and alpha (AOA—angle of attack). One of the standard jokes among pilots goes: "Flying's easy. Pull back on the stick and the houses get smaller. Push forward and the houses get larger." The houses are definitely getting smaller, fast.

The pilot and RSO must be in complete sync. They have the kind of trust that comes from years of rigorous training and a grueling selection process of candidates. Typically, pilots selected for the SR-71 program were highly experienced, with over 3,000 total hours in two or more aircraft. Fast mover (figher) time and air refueling experience were considered necessary in order to handle the intensive SR-71 training regimen and the aircraft itself, particularly in an operational environment.

RSOs frequently had similar experience with less total time. It was helpful for the RSO to have a fighter background because he had to perform many copilot-type duties as well as systems and navigation responsibilities. Experience in an aircraft where the navigator had a set of flight controls and a window seat proved valuable in helping an RSO develop the right mental attitude for this unusual airplane. He had to think like a pilot during some very crucial moments in flight, especially during emergencies.

Blackbird aircrews were volunteers. Roughly, four percent of the applicants would be called out for a week-long interview, with half of those selected for the program. Consequently, over its twenty-five-year history, the

Pappas and Manzi seated in the Blackbird. The crew was strapped into Martin-Baker ejection seats which were rated with a zero/zero capability, meaning that a survivable ejection could take place while the aircraft was sitting still on the ground. There were attachments on the S1030's boots with inertial reel cables that rapidly pulled the crew's feet back against the seat immediately prior to ejection.

number of men who flew the Blackbird operationally is quite small. The grueling interview consisted of two days of exhaustive physical examination, which had caused a number of aircrew members to be grounded—some permanently. The third day was spent in the SR-71 simulator. After a thirty-minute scan of the cockpit and switches, you were basically thrown to the wolves, flying the thing with multiple malfunctions heaped upon you for eight hours. When that was over you were tired, frustrated and had no idea whether you had done well or not. The fourth day included two flights in a Northrop T-38 Talon, a supersonic fighter-type jet used for training. One flight was flown with the squadron commander and the other with the Chief SR-71 Flight Examiner.

I was a little nervous, since I hadn't flown a stick (fighter-type cockpit) in over nine years. But my early career experience as a T-38 IP (instructor pilot) allowed me to settle in quickly and fly well. The last day of the week was spent in numerous one-on-one interviews with the wing commander and the senior staff. Basically, you needed a thumbs up from every person you encountered during the entire week in order to make the cut. The examination was the most thorough and grueling professional evaluation I can imagine. After waiting two months, the biggest professional thrill of my life was when I was notified I had qualified.

John Manzi, my RSO, and I started our year-long training program with a T-38 check out, lasting a few weeks, and we began to fly together as a crew. This very cost-effective airplane was used as a supplement in order to maintain our basic flying proficiency, such as instrument approaches and landings and developing our crew coordination. Then came two months of SR-71 academics to learn the aircraft systems, followed by four months of the most demanding simulator training I can think of. It was not fun. Some guys actually hate their instructors, still. They made it as hard on us as they possibly could because they knew that, eventually, we'd be on our own and responsible for a mission of top national importance and an airplane considered to be an irreplaceable national asset. Six months and 200 simulator hours into the training, we got to strap on a real Blackbird. It was worth the wait!

One of the special challenges of the early flight phase was learning to fly in the bulky, fifty-pound Dave Clark pressure suit. In order to keep the blood sugar level up, it was important to eat and drink during a mission. We ate things like apple sauce or, my favorite, peaches, from metal tubes with six inch plastic probes screwed onto one end (the food was made by Gerber and cost $20 per tube). I never had the courage to try the clam chowder. You would insert your tube food or water bottle probe through a sealed hole in the helmet and squeeze it into your mouth.

Once the early feelings of claustrophobia passed, you learned to

Essential to any SR-71 mission was aerial refueling, and the SR's needs were ably administered by a fleet of KC-135Q Stratotankers operated by the 100th Air Refueling Wing, also based at Beale. One of the Stratotankers (wearing the USAF's newer drab camouflage colors) is seen undergoing maintenance inside the 100th's hangar. Prominent is its huge refueling boom.

The graceful shape of a Blackbird climbing out from Beale. The pilot applies lateral pressure to the stick as he rolls into a turn to intercept the tanker. Almost all Blackbird missions took off with less than full tanks to improve performance, ensure a lighter load in the event of an emergency, and reduce stress on the airframe. This necessitated an early meeting with a KC-135Q from the 100th ARW. First refuelings usually took place at .9 Mach at 24,000 ft.

be comfortable in your custom-fitted $120,000 cocoon of a suit. Two Physiological Support Division (PSD) technicians were required to help a crew member don the suit, with a third supervisor technician inspecting their work. Our lives were literally in their hands. A sudden loss of cockpit pressurization at the altitudes we operated would cause a crew member's blood to boil instantly without the protection of that suit.

The last six months of the year were filled with increasingly challenging mission profiles in the aircraft and the simulator, until finally the newest SR-71 crew, coded number R-12, Pappas and Manzi, was certified mission ready and qualified for overseas deployment. It was November 1986 and we were ready to take the Blackbird out by ourselves to the ends of the earth.

With each subsequent takeoff, John and I appreciated the grueling training and our complete trust in each other's capabilities. Our communication was succinct but complete. Two minutes after takeoff, John would hear me say "burners" as I pulled the throttles out of afterburner. This was a courtesy to the RSO so he wasn't startled by the rather rough jolt as the afterburners were ignited or extinguished. After slowly pushing the stick forward to level off at 24,000 feet and 0.9 Mach, we flew toward the air refueling track. Usually, we would take

Because the SR-71 accelerates so rapidly, the gear has to be retracted immediately after takeoff. Rotation takes place at 210 knots and retraction takes place quickly once in the air so that gear retraction speed is not exceeded—an event that could cause damage to the airframe.

off with less than full fuel tanks, which gave us better aircraft performance and a wider safety margin in the event of an emergency, such as an engine failure during the critical takeoff phase. John was busy checking our reconnaissance and navigation equipment and making sure we were on the black line (flight planned route), as we approached the air refueling fix where a couple of KC-135Q tankers were orbiting. The tanker crews knew the location of the point we were flying to and coordinated their timing so their orbit coincided with our arrival. Our tanker crews were the best in the business. They accomplished this demanding rendezvous impressively—time and time again.

Sometimes we were very low on fuel after a high speed portion of the mission (hot leg), in which warmer than standard temperatures at high altitudes may have caused a greater use of fuel than was planned. After descending in bad weather at night and really cutting it close on fuel, those tankers looked awfully good when you finally made visual contact. I couldn't relax though until I was up under the tanker and felt the air refueling probe plug into the jet and could confirm that our fuel gauges were rising. That meant we were taking on fuel and wouldn't have to land in a foreign country.

Since nearly the entire body of the aircraft is full of fuel at full tanks, the tanker boom operators who plug us in the air often comment about the fluid appearance of the SR-71 as it flexes in waves while maintaining close formation position during the demanding air refueling maneuver. The cumulative effect of multiple refuelings and a long flight cocooned in our pressure suits is exhausting. Considerable mental fatigue accompanies flying 2,000 mph while watching the airplane like a hawk in order to react instantly to a problem before the situation has time to deteriorate. Making sure this potential for disaster is controlled is one of the most rewarding things about flying the SR-71.

Another motivation for my interest in flying the Blackbird was the fact that we routinely flew actual operational missions used for decision making by the highest national command

authorities. People were counting on us to do a difficult job under difficult circumstances. In a jet that was designed to operate routinely on the edge of the envelope, multiple malfunctions can quickly require that your knowledge, skill, reactions, communication and crew coordination click flawlessly. Often, it had to be flawless in order to keep from going outside the envelope permanently. The teamwork required to fly this machine successfully is extraordinary. The missions performed made it absolutely necessary. Virtually all of our work activities were done as a team for five years. We could practically read each other's mind and this really paid off when dealing with in-flight emergencies, sometimes a thousand miles from the nearest landing site.

Flying military is different from flying civilian. Civilian operations are generally designed to be in the middle of the envelope of possible performance, with large safety margins built in. The military is frequently driven by mission requirements to operate much closer to the edge of the envelope of available performance. This is not to say that military supervisors aren't safety conscious. They are. It just means that military aircrews must be more vigilant in their attention to detail. It is also more exciting to fly on the edge than in the middle and if it is being on the edge and excitement you are after, then there is no other ride like the Blackbird. Every system on board this magnificent machine was driven to its technological limit, and the crew members run up against their own physiological limits as well.

There is one mission John and I will never forget. It lasted over eleven hours—three times the length of an

With its position lights on, a KC-135Q and an SR-71A fly in dramatic formation. Fifty-six KC-135As were modified to Q configuration to support the SR-71 mission. The easiest way to spot a Q is by the single TACAN antenna used for SR rendezvous. The fuel system of these aircraft was also modified to accept the JP-7 burned by the Blackbird. Normally, a large percentage of the KC-135Qs would be based at Beale, but other planes would be dispersed to Blackbird operating locations around the world.

average flight. Five air refuelings were required, most of which were accomplished in extreme instrument conditions. The bad weather, combined with distance requirements and a tanker boom malfunction, forced me to maintain the air refueling contact position (close formation) for a cumulative total of three and one-half hours. Operational considerations in the target area forced us into aircraft performance regions never encountered on previous flights nor practiced in the simulator.

If all this wasn't bad enough, nine hours into the mission, I was temporarily blinded, presumably due to the 100-percent oxygen environment and the effects of my pressure suit helmet faceplate heater getting too hot. Reading my cockpit instruments was impossible. They were only a blur. I fought to suppress my rising panic. I remember saying to the Blackbird, "Please don't go haywire on me now."

My mind raced for ways to overcome the problem and the fear. Opening the helmet's faceplate to rub my eyes was tempting, but that move would prove fatal if we lost cabin pressure while it was open. I would have tried it if nothing else had worked. Fortunately, squinting hard for a few minutes, which seemed like forever, brought the desired results—tears. That moisture was just what my eyes needed, and they were the sweetest tears I've ever know. It is hard to describe my emotion as vision returned. Extreme relief mixed with concern that this problem could recur, and that it might not be so brief next time. I didn't tell John about the incident until we were safely on the ground. There was no sense in him sharing that helpless feeling with me unless absolutely necessary.

Two hours later, we completed the mission with a night landing that had all the flavor of a genuine emergency

With the boom plugged in, the SR-71 takes on a vital load of JP-7 so that the mission can continue. The tankers' crews knew just how vital fuel would be to a departing or returning Blackbird and mission rendezvous were planned to the exact second. The professionalism of the 100th ARW's crews was second to none.

procedure. Too exhausted to get out of the aircraft without help, I had tears in my eyes again as we shut it down and got out to the cheers of 120 maintenance and support technicians, many of them pushing a twenty-hour day. It was reportedly one of the most successful and important flights ever flown by the Blackbird. We were proud to help accomplish it, but any of the dozen crews in the squadron would have done the same thing. Habu tradition, the mission, the machine, and the men and women all combined for some powerful inspiration.

Most flights, however, were routine. As surprising as it may seem, breaking the sound barrier in modern aircraft is hardly noticeable unless you're watching your airspeed, altimeter and vertical velocity instruments. These will jump due to pressure changes as the shock wave slides aft along the aircraft's surface. In the SR-71, we also get a considerable shift aft in the center of lift, which causes a heavy nose down tendency. We will frequently use a climb and descent maneuver called the dipsy, to minimize the time and fuel used to make it through the Mach. Once the aircraft gets through that transsonic range with its associated high aerodynamic drag, just trim off the stick pressure and it is off to the races.

As you might guess, the world looks quite beautiful from 80,000 feet. There are no clouds obscuring the view and you can see for hundreds of miles. The sky is a deep dark blue, almost black at times. You can actually see the curvature of the earth. I've seen multiple sunrises and sunsets on more than one mission. Sometimes, however, I have been so occupied on a mission that I couldn't take a moment to look out at the incredible view.

The acceleration phase is one of the most challenging in the Sled (rocket

When returning from a mission, the Blackbird crew would start a gradual letdown at about 500 feet per minute (fpm) to allow for airframe cooling. Depending on the type of mission, another refueling might have taken place during the descent. A returning Blackbird would be loaded with information, its sensors being able to cover about 100,000 square miles of territory per hour.

46

Depending on the mission, the SR crew would sometimes treat the ground personnel at Beale, Kadena, Mildenhall and other OLs with a blazing afterburner pass. British citizens living in and around RAF Mildenhall had accepted the SR as one of their own. The Blackbird's final departure was an occasion of sadness.

sled), because everything is in a state of rapid flux. The engines must go through some dynamic changes as does the remarkable inlet system that allows for a movable spike in front of each engine. By decelerating part of this Mach 3-plus air, sending it through the jet engines and diverting much of it around the engines to be used in the afterburner section, we create a ram jet effect. As the aircraft gains speed, the spike in front of each engine is moved aft to control precisely the placement of the shock wave in front of the engine. The inlet is now started and running. At higher mach, we actually get more thrust from the inlet than from the engine and afterburner combined. Aerodynamic disturbances in an inlet are called an unstart, which means we will lose control of the shock wave on that engine and can instantly experience a violent asymmetric thrust condition that allows the canopy of the aircraft to slap one side of your head, hard, followed by severe turbulence, erratic attitudes and rapid altitude and

Over the final ten years of Blackbird operations, the type's safety record improved dramatically and only one aircraft was lost—an SR-71A that went down in the South China Sea in April 1989 following an engine unstart. After valiant efforts to save the craft, pilot Dan House and RSO Blair Bozek ejected and came down in the ocean. They had been able to broadcast their position prior to abandoning the Blackbird, and rescue forces were immediately on the way. However, the crew was rescued by native fishermen who took the parachuting airmen as an everyday event. The local chieftain's new throne is Dan House's ejection seat!

airspeed changes. In other words, all hell breaks loose until you can analyze the problem and get everything back under control. Failure to recover the inlet, even after taking manual control could mean a long, bumpy ride down to safer altitudes and airspeeds.

These are no longer frequent problems on the Blackbird like they were in its developmental years. With the best maintenance support in the world, this aircraft is incredibly reliable. It does, however, require a tremendous amount of logistical and maintenance expertise. Each flight was like a land speed record run at the Great Salt lakes. A lot of preparation went into making sure the aircraft and associated equipment were ready to go the speed of a rifle bullet at the top one percent of the atmosphere. The people who designed, built and supported this machine deserve a lot of credit and they are, understandably, very proud.

At the formal retirement ceremony at Beale AFB, California, Ben Rich, one of the men who helped Kelly Johnson design and build the SR-71, made a special point about the Blackbird's history. The SR-71, said Rich, was the only operational aircraft in USAF history not to have seen the loss of an Air Force aircrew member's life, nor to have been shot down in combat. After twenty-five years of unmatched service, the Blackbird went out at the top.

For twenty-five years the SR-71 Blackbird did things no other aircraft could do. It helped perform missions of the highest order for the United States and the Free World. A world rapidly expanding due, in part, to the contributions of this historic program. When reflecting on the many

Previous page
Over the northern California farmland, a Blackbird turns short final for the Beale runway. Lowering the landing gear helps cool the tires that have heated up during the high-speed portion of the mission. Touchdown is usually around 150 to 155 knots.

Their last Blackbird mission having come to an end in January 1990, Pappas and Manzi share a personal moment before departing their aircraft.

accomplishments of the Blackbird, it is important to remember the people—the men and women—whose dedication and hard work supported the operation and made it all happen, not just the few who were lucky enough to have flown it operationally.

Upon completion of their first operational mission, each new aircrew entered the ranks of those who had gone before them. They each became a Habu, the name of the cobra-like snake common to the island of Okinawa. When the natives there first glimpsed this strange looking black machine in the mid-60s, they pointed and exclaimed, "Habu! Habu!" because it reminded them of the deadly black snake. It was a tremendous sense of satisfaction and professionalism—I can think of no greater thrill in this business.

This information answers just some of the questions about this unique airplane, its crew members and what it was like to fly the Blackbird. Certain information about the SR-71 program remains classified. Perhaps some day all of the questions can be answered. As the Habus say, "Check twelve." Fly safe.

After the last flight, the ground crew carefully checks out the aircraft to make sure no damage was incurred during the mission. The inspection took several hours even though the Blackbird's next flight would probably be a one-way trip to a museum.

Final Flight

Beale Air Force Base is located in open countryside, north of the state capital of Sacramento, California. Large even by Strategic Air Command standards, Beale is clearly marked by the futuristic PAVE PAWS structure that houses an advanced sea-launched ballistic missile detection and warning system. Operated by the 7th Missile Warning Squadron, Air Force Space Command, PAVE PAWS is designed to give a few minutes vital warning in case of a surprise Soviet submarine missile bombardment.

More importantly, at least to the military aircraft enthusiast, Beale is also home to the 9th SRW, which operated (until the first part of 1990) two of Lockheed's finest products: the U-2R and TR-1 Dragon Lady and the mighty SR-71 Blackbird. The vast expanse of Beale keeps strategic intelligence gathering aircraft away from prying eyes as they go about their training flights or missions to remote operating locations (OLs).

Without a doubt, the SR-71 was the USAF's best-known and most readily identifiable aircraft to the general public. The same is also true for our nation's enemies. It has been estimated (officially) that SR-71s have been fired at well over 1,000 times with missiles during the course of strategic reconnaissance gathering missions. The fact that the Blackbirds have never been hit by enemy fire says a lot for the skill of the crews and the abilities of the aircraft.

SR-71A 960 sits proudly on the Beale AFB ramp a few days before the official final flight of the Blackbird in USAF service.

However, January 1990 was a particularly dark month for the personnel of the 9th SRW since the Blackbird was being permanently retired from the inventory of the USAF. Although Blackbird operations had not been funded by the USAF for the past two years, Congressional committees saw to it that needed money was forthcoming for operations.

Certain very high-placed officers in the USAF wanted the Blackbird gone—and gone quickly, especially before said officers' retirement. It was obvious that these critics of the Blackbird felt that if the aircraft was not retired before they retired, then there was a very good chance the machine would continue to operate with the USAF and that was not, in their minds, an acceptable situation. At this juncture, it is difficult to separate the reasons for the Blackbird's retirement: Was the move partially motivated by cost cutting, the aircraft being obsolete for the mission, or by a deeper, darker and more personal vendetta that did not regard the overall security of the United States as more important than personal ambition and desire?

"What air force would withdraw the world's fastest, highest flying aircraft and then state such an aircraft did not have a military mission within the overall USAF structure?" questioned one 9th SRW pilot during January.

"Handling of the SR-71 by the Air Force has been lackluster and unenthusiastic," was the comment from the House Armed Services Committee.

"Unenthusiastic, my ass!" was the retort from a Blackbird backseater. "I'd like to see one of those bloated bureaucrats put their fat ass in my seat

Lt. Col. Rod Dyckman (right) and Lt. Col. Tom Bergam share one last personal moment in 960's hangar before strapping in for final checks prior to the 26 January 1990 flight.

and go on some of the recent missions we've flown."

It appears that the Committee's comments were directed by information supplied directly from the USAF's highest officials and certainly did not take the actual professionalism of the crews and their missions into consideration before making a rather incredible statement.

In October 1989, a rumor circulated that the SR-71 force would be transferred to the Air National Guard. In a way, this made sense because the Guard has been tasked with more and

more specialized missions during recent years—including the air defense of the continental United States. The Senate Armed Services Committee, long supporters of the SR mission, wanted to transfer the program to the ANG along with $210 million in operational funds.

A meeting took place between the Senate and House committees and an agreement was worked out to place the Blackbird in other hands that would "more aggressively realize [the SR-71's] capabilities."

At this time, the two committees also agreed to funding an advanced reconnaissance system that was classified at the time and remains so today (this leads one to conjecture if the system was to be operated in space or if it was the oft-rumored Aurora, follow-on to the Blackbird). Money in the form

of $130 million was set aside for this mysterious program.

In a report on the conference, the following statement was made: "The Administration's [George Bush, President] budget request abandoned airborne reconnaissance, giving up on major present assets, principally the SR-71 aircraft system, and forgoing future ones [Author's note: Which, if true, would seem to end any thought of an Aurora-type aircraft], without any explanations of such draconian decisions. To describe such cuts as 'budgetary' begs vital questions about the wisdom of administration planning on key elements of the nation's intelligence capabilities."

Political fine points soon entered the picture, however, and the question was raised on how money could be supplied for systems that had not been

As 960 prepares to leave its hangar, the crew chiefs open the doors on all SR-71 hangars on the Beale line.

further authorized. At this point it seems that both committees just gave up on both the SR-71 and the classified advanced project. But, as previously stated, this could be deceiving.

During the latter part of 1989, some last minute attempts were apparently made by high-placed politicians to save the program, but nothing came of the efforts. The rapidly changing scenario in the communist nations of the world, combined with decreasing defense budgets, caused these voices to fall upon deaf ears.

At this point, it should be interjected that the SR-71 was *not*

operated solely for the benefit of the USAF although that organization did eventually gain a good deal from the results of the gathered information. The intelligence gathered by the SR-71's cameras and sensors went to the Central Intelligence Agency, Defense Intelligence Agency and US Navy. As a matter of course, these organizations received the data from requested Blackbird missions free of charge.

There is no doubt that the SR-71 was an expensive tool to operate. No published figure exists as to the direct operating costs of the limited production aircraft, but it was high—with estimates ranging from $150,000 to $250,000 per hour—when all costs (including tankers and associated support systems) were factored into the equation. However, the figure does not seem all that high when one considers

that the aircraft provided information linked directly to the defense of this nation.

Detractors of the SR-71 program point out that our increasing network of reconnaissance satellites can perform the aircraft's mission in a more satisfactory and less costly manner. There is some truth to that statement for, once the satellite is in position, the unit is fairly cost effective. However, the cost of building the satellite and putting the unit into orbit is very high.

There are a couple of main problems with satellites. One is the question of vulnerability since the Soviets have perfected an anti-satellite weapon system, and a satellite could do little to avoid a barrage of destructive weapons. A second problem is that of positioning: If a satellite is not in direct orbit over a particular area or problem

The Beale AFB tower, which has stood guard and monitored many classified Blackbird missions, silently watches over preparations for the last official SR-71 flight.

With J58s running, 960 is guided from its hangar with the same care as countless others from previous Blackbird missions. With a small burst of power, Lieutenant Colonel Dyckman taxis 960 from the hangar while a large crowd of well-wishers and media watch.

spot, it has to be positioned to provide needed information. If the satellite network has been damaged or if some units are inoperative, obvious problems arise.

With the sensor systems, both the SR and satellites have similar capabilities but the SR-71 is a much more flexible platform than are space vehicles. Maneuvering a satellite for coverage of a particular hot spot, such as in the crisis in Kuwait, might take several days and time is obviously critical during such a fast-moving event. An SR-71 probably could achieve the desired results in one mission. Given the Blackbird's speed, endurance and coverage capabilities, few parts of the world were far away. Regular Blackbird detachments (Dets) were maintained in Okinawa (Det. 1) and RAF Mildenhall, England (Det. 4). These detachments offered permanent bases for the SRs and were stocked with spares and dedicated maintenance personnel. SR-71s could be quickly readied for missions from these Dets to cover hot spots. Also, other more temporary Dets were maintained in different parts of the world and additional SR-71s could have been dispatched from Beale AFB in short notice.

Satellites have established a record of not being able to cover hot spots due to orbiting location, maintenance problems, and weather conditions. In such cases, Blackbirds were dispatched to cover these problems.

One pilot who had performed a crucial and very confidential mission within eighteen months before final phase-out felt that a satellite would not have been able to obtain the desired results within a very fixed time period. "We had to get results out of a hostile environment. It was a twelve-hour mission and some of these hours were spent hanging on the back of a tanker. We got the results, the mission was accomplished and the satellites could not have done it. I could hardly move my arms after the flight and had to be helped from the cockpit. Bitter? Sure, I'm bitter. I'm not pleased about a

career change but I am less pleased about leaving what I see as a gaping hole in the defense of my country."

It does not appear, at this time, that an advanced strategic reconnaissance aircraft will follow the SR-71. Gen. John Loh recently denied the existence of an Aurora-type aircraft by saying, "We do not have a Project Aurora." Such a statement, however, does not deny the existence of an advanced aircraft, it just denies something named Project Aurora. One

can easily recall the USAF denials over an aircraft called the F-19. They were right in denying the designation since the aircraft was really the Lockheed F-117A.

During 1990, many talks with representatives of major powers have been held concerning a new Open Skies policy. Veteran political observers may well remember that during the early 1950s, President Dwight D. Eisenhower proposed such a program to the Soviets. American aircraft would be allowed to overfly the Soviet Union to monitor troop and armament buildups and the Soviets would have the same privilege over the United States.

The Soviet government became quite frantic over this proposal and the result was that Kelly Johnson and his

Lockheed team built a new aircraft, a plane that was to eventually become known as the U-2.

The fact that Open Skies is once again upon us does, apparently, denote a new period of better relations between the world's two major military powers. But "just because you have a warm day in January does not mean you throw away your overcoat," said a USAF general who was also a supporter of the Blackbird program.

After weeks of agonized speculation, the official word came through that the SR-71 program would be closed down on 26 January 1990. Once the pronouncement came through, work began to rapidly phase the aircraft out of service. A few currency flights were undertaken to

Ben Rich enthusiastically greets the crew
while USAF officials look on.

Next page
Media representatives quickly surround 960
and its crew after the plane's arrival back at
Beale. The phasing out of the SR-71 fleet
made worldwide headlines.

SR pilot Lt. Col. Dan House conducted the phase-out ceremony in a clear-voiced, professional style but it was evident that much emotion was just under the surface.

make sure the pilot and RSO force was being maintained up until final phaseout.

A subdued ceremony was planned on the twenty-sixth but most of the pilots and RSOs of the 9th SRW felt cheated. "It's interesting to note that in the latest promotion lists, not one of our people remaining with the SR program was promoted. That is very unusual. Usually, a high percentage of our people up for promotion would be promoted. I think we have become an albatross around the USAF's neck," said a 9th RSO.

On the twenty-sixth, Lt. Col. Rod Dyckman and Lt. Col. Tom Bergam suited up in their Dave Clark full pressure suits and took a PSD van to their waiting SR-71A, number 960, sitting in its protective Beale hangar. Family members and other spectators were on hand for a brief ceremony at the aircraft before the crew strapped in. Fueled by a shot of tetraethyl borane (TEB—used to lower the high flash point of the special JP-7 fuel), the mighty Pratt & Whitney J58s were started and the SR trundled out of its hangar and headed to the runup area as supporters, the general public, and the media observed.

Once final checks were completed, Lieutenant Colonel Dyckman took the runway and another squirt of TEB got the afterburners going, shooting out the characteristic diamond shock patterns, and the SR-71 headed down Beale's long runway.

In the meantime, officials had arrived at the base in a variety of aircraft (several who were directly responsible for the aircraft's retirement) and a platform was set up where appropriate speeches could be made to the personnel of the 9th and the media.

Shortly before 1600 hours, Lieutenant Colonel Dyckman brought 960 over Beale at altitude and at Mach 3-plus, resulting in a satisfying sonic boom. Dyckman and 960 returned to make several impressive passes, some in conjunction with an accompanying T-38 chase plane before landing.

After landing, the crew departed the aircraft and was greeted by officials. They then went to the reviewing stand where several speeches were made—some heartfelt, some not. "This is garbage, pure garbage," commented one veteran SR-71 driver as his eyes teared over.

SR-71 co-designer and head of the Lockheed Skunk Works, Ben Rich, made a moving speech about the Blackbird and its capabilities but, in a few short moments, the end of an era had taken place, leaving those who had flown, maintained and supported the SR-71s a bit stunned.

"The planes were over twenty years old," said one ranking USAF official. "They were getting tired, parts were hard to come by—it was time for the boneyard."

"Nonsense," snapped a Blackbird technician. "The airplanes are in better condition than ever and the parts situation is actually the best it has ever been. Every time an SR-71 flies, the titanium structure heats up and cools down—making the entire airplane tougher and tougher after each flight. The SR-71 is the only twenty-five-year-old aircraft in the USAF inventory that has not suffered from wing cracks."

On the evening of the retirement day, a ceremony and dinner was held in the Beale Officers' Club. It was a strange affair. Many prominent people who had flown and supported the

The look on Lieutenant Colonel Dyckman's face expresses his feeling as the Blackbird flag is retired. As a point of interest, the Blackbird flag was purchased by the crews since USAF officials had little interest in supplying anything to do with the final ceremony.

SR-71s over the years were present. Some of the individuals who helped usher the aircraft out of service were also in attendance and the applause meter left no doubt who was in favor and who wasn't as each guest was introduced. "This is a wake, not a party," said one speaker to the assembled group. The mood was unpleasant and somber.

When Ben Rich made his speech, he stated, "This year [1990] the Rockwell B-1B Lancer will achieve the same stealth footprint that the SR-71 has had for twenty-five years." This statement brought a solid round of applause and cheering from the assembled 9th SRW officers.

What of the aircraft? During the retirement, it appears that about thirteen aircraft were present at Beale including at least two damaged machines that were being used as "Christmas trees" for spare parts and the unique SR-71C which had not flown for years. "No one likes [the SR-71C]," said one crew chief. "It's a difficult machine to maintain and, according to the pilots, to operate."

Many SRs have been dispersed to museums but three planes have been transferred to NASA for possible future operations while several others are to be maintained in flyable condition for possible national emergencies. Some other aircraft are apparently slated for scrapping. "With that titanium structure, those sons of bitches are going to have a hard time cutting up our birds," said a crew chief.

As this book was being prepared for press (in September 1990), a high-ranking military official involved in the Gulf Crisis has publicly made statements that he needs intelligence that can only be provided by a Blackbird. Does the Gulf Crisis constitute, in the bureaucrats' minds, a national emergency? Will USAF Blackbirds fly again? It's difficult to say. As each week goes by, the chance becomes more remote as talent, parts and supplies get further and further apart.

As readers of this volume will see, the last official flight of the Blackbird was certainly not the type's last flight. Deliveries were made to NASA and various museums, and one plane made a headline-grabbing record flight. "It's bit curious that an aircraft already retired from the Air Force went on to break a record that may never again be broken," said one SR-71 pilot.

Curious indeed. But the Blackbird has always been one curious bird.

The Blackbird fleet is officially stood down and a most distinctive chapter in aviation history comes to a close.

The Big Picture

Before the SR-71 fleet was completely dispersed from Beale AFB, the authors came up with a plan to photograph the base's contingent of strategic reconnaissance Blackbirds in one group portrait. Needless to say, this request was greeted with rather blank stares in some quarters—especially from the people who had a vested interest in seeing that the Blackbird fleet was permanently grounded. What we wanted to do was preserve history on film—to create a photograph where Beale's Blackbird heritage was brought together in one place at one time.

However, the majority of the decision makers at Beale wanted the photograph, as did the ground crews who serviced the intelligence gathering aircraft so faithfully over the years. Eleven aircraft were available for the portrait after the foreign-assigned SRs had been brought back from their Dets. Several other Blackbirds located at the base were not in exactly presentable condition since they had been used as

The morning of the scheduled SR-71 group portrait dawned clear but quickly degenerated into fog and snow flurries in the nearby foothills. So much for advanced planning! The fog became so intense that the towing of the first two aircraft had to be stopped. One of the Blackbirds is seen here as a rather spectral image.

The photographers went through countless sheets of paper as they sketched out plans that would best illustrate the group portrait of Beale's Blackbirds. Since the SR is extremely long and narrow, grouping the aircraft for the portrait was not easy.

parts sources after being damaged in various incidents. These aircraft were left in the hangars. Several of the Blackbirds available for the photo had not flown in some time, although they had been kept in flyable storage.

One particularly interesting machine that had not seen the light of day for some time was the one and only SR-71C. A total of thirty-one SR-71s was produced and this does not include the C model, which picked up the unfortunate nickname "The Bastard." A need for a dedicated Blackbird crew trainer was soon realized as the fleet became operational and s/n 64-17956 was converted to SR-71B dual control trainer configuration with a rather ungainly hump of a fully instrumented second cockpit grafted onto the space previously occupied by the RSO. This machine has been well used in the training mission and has proven invaluable in dramatically reducing the SR accident rate. When the cancellation of Blackbird program became a reality, the SR-71B was undergoing deep maintenance at Palmdale.

Another SR-71B was created to help alleviate the training load on the first B but this aircraft was lost in an accident. Since the USAF had a finite number of SRs available and operational considerations had to be regarded first and foremost, a decision was made to create a third dual control trainer by a method that was both unique and totally unsatisfactory.

Over the years, bits and pieces from various crashed Blackbirds were closely hoarded and the rear portion of a YF-12A that had been written off at Edwards AFB was kept in storage. The problem of what to do for a forward section was solved when it was decided

As the sun began to rise a bit higher in the east, the fog began to disperse, allowing the continued towing of Blackbirds from their hangars. One of the planes is seen hooked to its powerful tug.

to use the SR-71A engineering mockup. This rather unorthodox combination was slowly pieced together as engineers tried to figure out how to match up divergent wiring and systems.

The resulting creation was called the SR-71C and given the serial number 64-17981. Right from the start the plane was less than popular with the maintenance folks and pilots alike. Working on the plane was extremely

difficult because the majority of the systems were lash-ups and did not conform to the regular SR maintenance program. Pilots found the aircraft "different" to fly—somewhat like an automobile that has been badly repaired following an accident and drives out of alignment. It did not take long before the Charlie Model was shoved into a hangar and left. The plane was not even particularly heavily cannibalized for extra parts. The SR-71C shared space with another SR-71A that had been damaged after an engine unstart and was being picked to pieces. There was at least one other (and possibly two) Blackbird that had been used for spares and this aircraft

was left in the hangar because it was decidedly unphotogenic.

Our mass portrait exercise began early one cold February 1990 morning at Beale. The day had dawned clear but heavy snowfall was occurring in the nearby Sierra foothills. Our meeting with the ground crew and some of the higher ranking officers went smoothly and our plan for positioning the aircraft was presented and agreed upon by all concerned. It was time to get moving but after we exited the building, all of us were surprised to find the base blanketed by an extremely dense layer of fog that completely blotted out the sun! Beale is located in an area of California that is often beset

Hooked to its tug, a Blackbird is moved to its assigned parking space. The dedicated ground crews had to put up with dozens of minute positioning changes until the Blackbirds were perfectly aligned for the cameras.

71

SR-71A 64-17976 displays the chalked portrait of a large tiger on its verticals. The temporary nature of the chalk usually meant that the artwork would last only a couple of flights.

As it is towed to position, this SR-71A displays its stripped out sensor bays—a sign that the fleet was already being deactivated.

by dense fog—a situation that, during the winter months, can last for days.

Two Blackbirds had already been pulled from their hangars for positioning and were stopped in place until the weather improved. At one point, the fog became so intense that it was almost impossible to see more than a few feet and the headlights on the tugs became just feeble spots of light. Fortunately, as the sun rose higher in the sky, the fog began to move and disperse—oddly covering one end of the base in murk while leaving our area in bright sunshine with a beautiful blue sky.

The remaining part of the moving and positioning of aircraft went smoothly, thanks to the enthusiasm of the ground crew. It was not an easy task because the Blackbird is a very large aircraft that has to be slowly and carefully moved. This problem was also compounded by the fact that the aircraft were being positioned extremely close together and utmost care was needed by the drivers of the tugs and the ground directors.

Slowly, the big picture started coming together and after about four hours of hard work, Eric Schulzinger climbed into a USAF cherry picker and headed up sixty feet to take the group portrait. Needless to say, the movement of this many aircraft around the base had attracted a lot of interest, and after our work was completed, the base personnel were allowed to inspect the gathering of eleven of Lockheed's finest. For the most part, the spectators were silent as they wandered through the rows of what was once America's most secret aircraft. They all realized that an important era in aeronautical history was rapidly drawing to a close. The majority of SR pilots and RSOs avoided the group portrait. They all knew very few of them would again fly their favorite aircraft—and those flights would be one-way subsonic missions to museums.

As we packed our camera gear away, the ground crews began the task of moving their charges back into the hangars. A moment in history had passed but at least it had been recorded on film for posterity.

For the first time in years, SR-71C is brought from its hangar. This aircraft was created by mating the rear portion of wrecked YF-12A 60-6934 to the front of the engineering mockup of an SR-71A. The SR-71C was used as a dual-control trainer, much like the SR-71Bs, but maintenance of the plane was a nightmare since the wiring and many of the systems did not conform to the rest of the fleet. The SR-71C carries the serial 64-17981 and features the old style SR markings with large national insignia, serial in white and a buzz number on the nacelle.

The aircraft start coming together as personnel in the Beale tower watch. "I had no idea we had that many Blackbirds stuffed away in hangars," commented one officer. Some of the SRs had not flown in years.

Just as the maintenance crews did not like
the SR-71C, the pilots also had an aversion
to flying the craft because its handling
qualities were not particularly pleasant. It
did not take long before the SR-71C became
a hangar queen, sharing space with another
SR-71A that had suffered an engine unstart
that damaged its wing structure and nacelle
beyond economical repair. Both planes
became sources for spare parts.

These are the men who put in many hard hours of moving Blackbirds for the group portrait.

Once the aircraft were in position, the photographer went up in a 60-foot cherry picker to record the event on film.

Previous page
As the Blackbirds come together, spectators begin to gather by the hundreds to see a sight that had never before been seen—and certainly would not occur again after the day was over.

The ramp begins to fill with black noses and fins while the tankers of the 100th Aerial Refueling Wing fill the background.

The final result was worth all the effort. Eleven of the 9th Strategic Reconnaissance Wing's Blackbirds pose for a stunning portrait. One or two other cannibalized SRs were left in their hangars.

This high-angle late-afternoon view of two of the SR-71As shows a curious silver-like reflection being given off by the iron-ball paint. Areas of repainting can also be seen in the highlights.

*The operational hopes for the Blackbirds
will be with NASA, who has obtained three
aircraft and a large quantity of spare parts
as well as the SR simulator.*

*Their sharp noses no longer pointing to the
future, these Blackbirds await assignment
to various museums across the country.*

An SR-71A is towed back into its hangar as
the historic gathering is dispersed forever.

A view from the tower as the sun sets on the
Blackbird fleet.

Each Blackbird had its own dedicated band of specialists led by a crew chief. Watching his aircraft coming out of its hangar, Steve

Koren is typical of the hardworking crew chiefs who kept the Blackbirds operational for response to any sort of crisis.

Blackbird People

All of the American Armed Services are staffed by dedicated, motivated volunteers. Each service has its own unique *esprit de corps,* but perhaps the most enthusiastic service is the United States Air Force. The USAF is also the youngest of all American armed services, established in 1947 following a proud tradition as the Army Air Force in World War II.

In today's Air Force, perhaps the most elite units are the Lockheed F-117A squadrons. Operating for nearly a decade in great secrecy from a base in Nevada, the F-117A was made public in 1990 and the proud pilots were finally able to display their strange-looking machines to the public and to their families. "It was kinda hard to leave your family each week and fly to a secret air base where all operations took place at night and were extremely classified. We couldn't even hint to our families at what we were flying or doing," said Col. Tony Tolin, commander of the 37th Tactical Fighter Wing—the parent unit that operates the Stealth Fighter squadrons and training unit.

The fact that Stealth pilots can now exhibit their aircraft at airshows and answer the barrage of questions from the public (for the record, the most commonly asked question is "where is the engine exhaust?") is great for morale. Before the unmasking of the Stealth Fighter, the USAF's most elite unit was the 9th Strategic Reconnaissance Wing, operator of the SR-71 Blackbird.

When the government allowed the Blackbird to begin visiting airshows, the plane and its crew were literally swamped by an enthusiastic and adoring public who wanted to ask every question and examine every inch of the world's most exotic military aircraft.

This was difficult because the aircraft was usually cordoned off and guarded by two to four security personnel while the pilot and RSO were strictly limited about what they could discuss with members of the public. However, the pride they took in their aircraft was easily distinguished.

The pride of the flight crews was not limited to just the pilots who took the SR-71 into the blackness of near space, it was a feeling that permeated

Every phase of the Blackbird's operation was closely controlled for accuracy and safety. A crewman is seen carefully guiding a returning SR-71 to its parking area.

every unit of the 9th SRW. From a first year airman to a commanding officer, pride in the unit, the aircraft, and the mission was an accepted fact in the 9th SRW.

Dedication extended from the crew chiefs and the maintenance specialists (both civilian and military) who worked long, hard hours to make sure the Blackbirds were ready to fly. Because of the mission, the men and women of the 9th regarded themselves as the "last of the individualists" and, to a great extent, this was true since so many of the 9th's missions were very self-contained.

Blackbird crews usually had a greater degree of freedom than other Strategic Air Command units because a major part of the mission was going off to Operating Locations and performing the required mission under a tight web of security.

All-important maintenance was performed on the Blackbirds by the men and women of the 9th Organizational Maintenance Squadron, who coped with the day-to-day requirements of the fleet. The 9th OMS handled the launch and recovery of the Blackbirds while performing repairs and maintenance of a more minor nature. In-depth maintenance was carried out by the 9th Field Maintenance Squadron and this type of work included intermediate repairs and refurbishment. Avionics repair and refurbishment was performed by the 9th Avionics Maintenance Squadron. The Precision Measurement Equipment Laboratory kept the classified sensors, navigation equipment, ECM packages, and communications gear in fine working order.

Each Blackbird mission generated a tremendous amount of intelligence

These men kept the Blackbird fleet at peak efficiency—the crew chiefs and specialists of the 9th Strategic Reconnaissance Wing. "SR-71 operational capability, maintenance and spare parts availability was at its best when the unit was shut down," commented one crew chief.

material and it fell to the men and women of the 9th Reconnaissance Technical Squadron to interpret this data. This was usually done in mobile vans stationed at each Operating Location and the completed data was then passed on to each mission's main customer—usually the Navy or the CIA. Further data interpretation was

also carried out by the ultra-secret 544th Strategic Intelligence Wing whose home base is at Offutt AFB in Nebraska.

The 9th Supply Squadron and Lockheed field services worked hand-in-hand to make sure that vital spare parts were on hand to keep the Blackbird fleet airworthy and to get a grounded SR back into the air with the least amount of time and trouble.

The Pratt & Whitney facility at West Palm Beach, Florida, would undertake the overhaul of the J58 engines as each powerplant reached the 600-hour operating mark. When the airframes themselves needed a complete overhaul, they were returned

to the Lockheed facility at Palmdale for a dedicated rebuild.

Field service representatives from P&W, Lockheed, and the many other companies that had equipment in the Blackbird were all stationed at Beale and at OLs and had to work long hours, often in a very hostile climate, to make sure that everything was up and running when the Blackbird was required for a mission.

The crews of the 100th Aerial Refueling Wing developed an unsurpassed reputation for being on station at the right time and right place to keep hungry Blackbirds well fed. In fact, the story of the 100th's tanker

After each SR-71 mission, the crew chief and his team would closely inspect the aircraft to make sure that everything was in operational order. In this photograph, the titanium afterburner section is minutely examined for possible cracks.

missions would fill up at least one very exciting large book.

The 9th Security Police Squadron was tasked with the mission of keeping the Blackbirds safe from possible attacks by terrorists or vandals. They performed their mission superbly and

the wording "use of deadly force authorized" on the many security signs surrounding the flight line was not to be taken lightly.

As can be seen, it took many different people from many different disciplines to keep the Blackbird fleet operating. The fact that America had the world's best intelligence system while the Blackbird fleet was flying is testimonial to the effectiveness of their combined talents.

Next page
Pilots and RSOs enjoy a moment of relaxation in the PSD van. The men and women of the Physiological Support Division made sure that the Blackbird crews were safely installed in their Dave Clark high-altitude S1030 suits.

Commanding officer of the 9th SRW Lt. Col.
Rod Dyckman (left) and RSO Lt. Col. Tom
Bergam with a Blackbird on the Beale ramp
shortly before the aircraft's last official
flight.

A PSD specialist makes a last minute helmet adjustment on the custom-fitted $120,000 S1030 suit. During SR-71 and TR-1 operations, PSD employed approximately 100 people. Getting into the suit required the help of two PSD specialists and took about twenty minutes. The pilot and RSO then had to breathe 100 percent oxygen for thirty minutes to eliminate nitrogen from their blood, thus reducing the possibility of bends.

In every Air Force unit there are usually one or two extremely talented artists and the 9th SRW was no exception. A maintenance sergeant displays his attractive dart board that had been chalked onto the tail of 64-17980, the last Blackbird built. One of the aircraft returning to Beale from a foreign Det had a large tombstone and RIP chalked on the tail. High-ranking officers found little humor in this art and ordered it removed before the retirement ceremony. Interestingly, Blackbirds were never washed since water getting inside the aircraft could spell trouble. Instead, a special cleaning solvent was used for the upkeep of the iron ball paint.

The Strategic Air Command takes security at all its bases very seriously but it took Beale security extremely seriously. The 9th Security Police Squadron is responsible for protecting the critical national defense assets based at Beale while also providing base residents with professional police services.

Lockheed's chief field representative at Beale, the man who kept Blackbird services running smoothly between the USAF and Lockheed and keeps the same service humming along for the TR-1 fleet is Fred Carmody. Fred was a World War II crew chief on Consolidated B-24 Liberators and has been deeply involved in aviation for all his adult life.

The operational pilots and RSOs of the 9th SRW pose with one of their aircraft before its retirement. The actual last flights made by Blackbirds took place as the airworthy Beale SRs were ferried to new homes at museums across the country.

In recent years, the Blackbird fleet had been particularly valuable in gathering information from hostile Third World countries like Cuba and Nicaragua. One knowledgeable source stated that to keep nine SRs operational with associated tankers and crews was equal to keeping two tactical fighter wings in Europe. However, crews like these were highly trained teams that always brought back results in short order—something that can't always be said of satellites and other intelligence gathering systems. Pilots and RSOs came from a wide variety of USAF flying backgrounds, but the goal of successfully accomplishing a difficult mission bound the 9th SRW into a tight family.

Going for the Gold

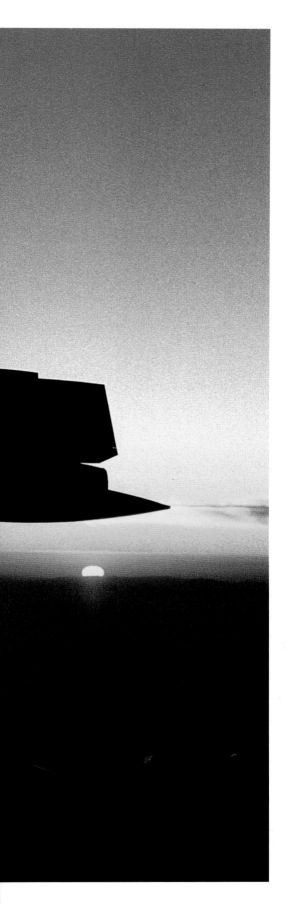

Nearly two months after the type was officially retired from United States Air Force service in ceremonies at Beale AFB, a Lockheed SR-71A set four international speed records while on a flight from the west to east coasts of the United States. The record flight had been cancelled at least once by top USAF officials who had no desire to see the event take place. It appears that the final record flight was pushed through by the muscle of certain Lockheed executives, politicians who were SR-71 supporters, and a small cadre of lower ranking but influential USAF officers who felt the record would enhance the USAF's position in the light of 1990's massive military budget cuts.

Even though the flight was finally approved to take place on 6 March 1990, USAF reticence nearly prevented media coverage of the aircraft's launch from Lockheed's Palmdale, California, Plant 42. Only last minute pressure by the media combined, once again, with pressure from certain USAF officers, allowed national live coverage of the important event to take place. In particular, CNN did a very good job of covering the record run along with providing some insightful comments about the SR-71. They also conducted interviews with individuals who had important ties to the nearly thirty-year-old program.

The aircraft chosen for the flight was SR-71A USAF s/n 64-17972, a

With the morning sun rising over the Los Angeles basin, SR-71A 972 began its speed run into the history books. The double sonic boom awoke thousands of residents in southern California.

veteran of previous SR-71 speed runs from the United States to the Farnborough Air Show in Britain. On 1 September 1974, Maj. Jim Smith and RSO Maj. Noel Widdifield piloted 17972 from New York to London in 1 hour, 54 minutes and 56 seconds, covering a distance of 3,490 miles and averaging 1807 mph.

On 13 September, Capt. Harold "Buck" Adams and RSO Maj. William C. Machorek took 17972 from London to Los Angeles, covering the 5,645 miles in 3 hours, 47 minutes and 36 seconds for an average speed of 1436 mph.

As a point of historical interest, 17972 made its first flight on 12 December 1966 and logged 2795.3 flying hours up until the time of its final record flight. The SR-71A accrued this time during 900 sorties, 197 of which were operational missions. This Blackbird had been stationed at Beale AFB on eighteen occasions during its lifetime, the first of which was on 3 March 1967. During its various tours at Beale, 17972 logged 237 sorties, five of which were operational.

The plane was also assigned to Det. 1 at Kadena Air Base in Okinawa (now part of Japan) on four occasions and flew fifty-three operational missions (mainly in support of the Vietnam War) from this strategically important base. This SR-71A also journeyed to RAF Mildenhall, England, on 20 April 1976 to mark a steady build-up of SR-71As at this field and form the permanent Det. 4. During the SR's service at Mildenhall, the Blackbird became identified with the English who thought of the plane as one of their own. In its log, 17972 shows 652 hours of flying time taking place on flights over three hours duration.

SR-71 17972 also spent a good deal of time at Plant 42 where it was used for test and development work. The plane was easily identifiable by the famed Lockheed Skunk Works insignia carried on the twin vertical fins, indicating the craft was assigned to Det. 6, the 2762nd Logistics Support Squadron (Special) at Palmdale. Det. 6 provided the logistics support for the Blackbird fleet and supervised Lockheed as the company performed major maintenance and modifications on the SR-71.

In addition, Det. 4 conducts flight tests, provides security, maintenance engineering and all other activities associated with the operating and maintaining of the U-2R and TR-1 fleet of aircraft. Det. 6 was originally part of the Air Force Systems Command (AFSC) at Mira Loma AFS but was relocated to San Bernardino Air Material Area, Norton AFB, and remained with AFSC until 1968.

In 1969, Det. 4 became Det. 51 and was transferred to the Air Force Logistics Command (AFLC). The detachment conducted flight tests of the SR-71 at Edwards AFB until October 1970 when AFSC relinquished test operations of AFLC and moved the test site to Plant 42. In 1977, the detachment was redesignated Det. 6, the 2762nd Logistics Support Squadron.

The Blackbird has also set other significant aerospace records. On 27 July 1976, an SR-71A set three records while flying over a 1,000 kilometer course (621.369 miles): an absolute and a class speed record of 2092.294 mph without a payload, and a class speed record of 2092.294 mph with a 2204.6-pound payload. Only 28 July, two world altitude records for horizontal sustained flight without payloads were set: An absolute and a class altitude record of 85,068.997 feet. Also on 28 July, another SR-71A set two world

The crew for the record-shattering flight consisted of pilot Lt. Col. R. Edward Yeilding (right) and RSO Lt. Col. Joseph T. Vida. Both men had considerable operational experience in the Blackbird, and Vida holds the record for most hours in an SR-71. The crew is seen at Palmdale's Plant 42 shortly before the record flight.

SR-71A 972 makes its arrival pass over the distinctive Dulles Airport control tower after shattering the cross-country speed record.

speed records in the last ten kilometers of a twenty-five kilometer straight course without payload: an absolute and a class speed record of 2193.16 mph.

Intense planning for the 6 March 1990 record flight was interrupted by USAF vacillation, including a concerted effort by the USAF Chief of Staff to terminate the flight. Morale was duly affected. Although the pilots and RSOs were reasonably glum, several USAF officials stated that they thought the coast-to-coast run could be made in just under one hour, a stunning record if captured.

Crew for the record flight consisted of Lt. Col. R. Edward Yeilding (more than ninety operational Blackbird missions) and RSO Lt. Col. Joseph T. Vida (chief of SR-71 flight test and highest flight time SR-71 crewmember with over 1,390 hours and ninety-five operational missions).

A predawn launch was successfully undertaken out of Palmdale followed by an aerial refueling. A slight delay was incurred when a problem developed over the amount of fuel transferred from the tanker, but this was soon rectified. Entering its first "gate" near Los Angeles, the SR-71A was accelerating through Mach 2.5 and climbing—laying down a sharp double sonic boom that made many workbound Los Angeles residents, alerted to the flight by the media, know the race was on.

The flight was monitored by the National Aeronautic Association, the US representative for the Federation Aeronautique Internationale, which is the international record keeper for such flights. The NAA had officials in Palmdale and Air Traffic Control Centers in Los Angeles, Kansas City, Indianapolis, Leesburg and Dulles

Strange sight. With all the airport's crash and rescue vehicles in tow, 972 taxis past a variety of airliners and civil aircraft as it heads for the reception area. Wonder what the passengers thought?

Ben Rich (left) provided live comments over CNN on the speed run.

The 6 March 1990 speed run would be 972's final flight. Over the next few days, the aircraft would be runup to dispose of fuel, other systems would be drained of liquids, the ejection seats disarmed and certain systems would be removed prior to storing the aircraft for future display in the National Air and Space Museum. The Blackbird taxis in for engine shut down in front of the press, ground crew and dignitaries.

Airport. Timing was accomplished through the use of air traffic control radar that could pinpoint the time over any point to less than one second.

The SR-71A was in stock condition but did not carry any sensor packages and the gate-to-gate flight was made without refueling. The closing gate was just off the east coast and the welcoming crowd at Dulles was able to hear a sonic boom as the aircraft

passed nearby. A dull, cloud-filled sky prevented any sighting of the SR-71's characteristic speeding pure white vapor trail. Once the final gate had been crossed, another refueling took place (the crew later stated that the aircraft had a good safety margin of fuel on board to land at Dulles but the refueling was carried out as an added safety precaution). The SR-71 then entered the Dulles airspace and made two lackluster passes over the field before settling in for a smooth landing.

The aircraft and crew were greeted by a small band of dignitaries that included Ben Rich, Dr. Martin Harwit (Director, National Air and Space Museum), Brig. Gen. Harold Adams (former SR-71 record setter and now deputy director for force structure and

resources, Joint Chiefs of Staff), Col. Eldon Joersz (assistant director for Joint and National Security Council matters and holder of the SR-71 absolute speed record in aircraft 958), Mal Gross (President, NAA), the Hon. John Warner (US Senator from Virginia and supporter of the SR-71 program), and Lynn Helms (former CIA director).

To illustrate just how bad the rift was between senior USAF commanders and the supporters of the Blackbird program, no senior USAF officers attended the event. The presence of these political opportunists was not missed according to several USAF officers interviewed off the record. This snub also accented personal ambitions holding importance over apparently

Yeilding and Vida display their National Aeronautic Association (the organization that monitored the cross-country run) certificates following the successful conclusion of the record-breaking run.

more minor matters like national security.

In a very brief ceremony, logs of the aircraft were handed over to the NASM and a few speeches were made. Dulles is the site of a proposed new NASM branch museum but it appears the SR-71 will have to sit outside in the terrible Dulles weather for several years before funding is at hand for protection of the airframe. Hopefully some Dulles hangar space can be found

so that the SR-71 does not have to suffer in the weather.

A short, uneasy press conference was held in a small airport office but little of importance was said except a statement by one of the crew that he was not convinced "satellites could handle the type of mission undertaken by the SR-71." A nervous USAF public relations representative quickly terminated the press conference with a lame excuse about the crew being "overheated."

The NAA stated the average speed set by the SR-71 was 2112.52 mph covering a distance of 2404.05 statute miles in 68 minutes and 17 seconds. Why the flight took over an hour was unexplained. Lieutenant Colonel Yeilding stated that the flight could

Next page
After Yeilding and Vida shut down the Blackbird and disembarked, a small welcoming committee made speeches (Ben Rich is at the podium) and 972's logs were transferred to the NASM.

have been made a few minutes faster if "certain parameters had been exceeded" but it was not considered worthwhile.

Perhaps the most fitting comments regarding the SR-71's retirement were made plane-side in an emotion-filled speech by General Adams, who said in a trembling voice, "Take care of her. She's a truly magnificent machine. And she's retiring a winner."

End of the Line

Visitors are not encouraged at the USAF's Plant 42 in Palmdale, California. The huge chunk of Mojave Desert land has been and still is home to many classified military projects. Palmdale is currently home for some interesting projects including the heavily-guarded Northrop B-2 Stealth Bomber manufacturing and assembly plant, the Rockwell B-1B modification and update center, and Lockheed's P-3 Orion manufacturing and TR-1 overhaul and maintenance facilities. The last few Orions are rolling off the production line built inside the huge hangar that was constructed to house the near-disastrous L-1011 airliner program.

The area is regularly patrolled and security is tight. For many years a hangar on the northern side of the field kept some highly classified aircraft hidden from public scrutiny: The surviving members of the Lockheed A-12 fleet that had been operated on clandestine missions by the CIA had been partially preserved and stuffed into one of the large hangars to avoid prying eyes and Soviet intelligence satellites. The aircraft were placed in storage sometime in the early 1970s but somewhere along the line funding for keeping the planes in the hangar ran out and the A-12s, along with a couple of preserved SR-71s, were towed outside and parked on the ramp—easily seen by overflying private aircraft or people driving on one of the many access roads in the area.

Breaking open the SprayLat seal, a Worldwide Aircraft Recovery Systems worker begins the long process of preparing a stored Blackbird for transportation to a new home.

Repeated requests to photograph the planes met with very definite negative replies even though the aircraft could basically be examined from a short distance by whomever.

Once in outside storage, there was no apparent attempt to perform any type of maintenance on the aircraft and even though some of the planes had a pretty healthy coating of SprayLat preservative, it was obvious even to the most casual observer that the aircraft were on a one-way trip downhill.

SR-71s often used Palmdale as they visited the facility for updates or deep maintenance work and it was not uncommon to have between three and four SRs at Palmdale at any given time, making for a rather strange contrast with the A-12s. The SR-71s had, of course, taken over the majority of the missions required by the CIA and the A-12s had little or no future but were apparently kept on hand in the event of some form of national emergency. However, since the condition of the A-12s had been allowed to deteriorate to such an extent, the emergency would probably have been long over before the first of the rebuilt A-12s would have been capable of flying!

So, for nearly two decades, the A-12 fleet has done a slow rot at Palmdale along with a couple of SRs that also had been grounded for nonspecific reasons—perhaps airframe damage or the simple fact the planes were surplus to requirements. It is possible that some applicable spares were stripped from these aircraft to become part of the SR spares pool because one Blackbird crew chief had made the statement that the Blackbird's spares situation was the "best it has ever been."

However, with the abrupt grounding of the Blackbird and the

This Blackbird is of interest because of the two different serials on the vertical tails. This probably came about as parts were swapped prior to disassembly.

warming of relations between the United States and the Soviet Union, reasons for the continued storage of the A-12 fleet became minimal. As the final,

sad days of Blackbird operations at Beale began to wind down with last flights being made to various museums and USAF displays around the country, the people behind the phaseout of Kelly Johnson's most magnificent creation wanted all traces of this fabulous flyer erased forever. The quick action of some concerned USAF officers, Lockheed employees, and private citizens

guaranteed that the Blackbirds would not become just a fond memory.

Ideally, it would have been wonderful if a few SR-71s could have been released as surplus and put on the US civil register. "With the correct operating procedures, the SR-71 would have made an ideal civilian contract vehicle," stated one former Blackbird driver. "The plane could have been

A dismembered wing section on its transport trailer. Note the neat job Worldwide did in taking the wing apart. Torrey Engineering assisted Worldwide in forming a plan to take the aircraft apart with the least amount of physical damage.

operated for a profit while providing valuable data to contractors such as private aerospace industry and universities." This, unfortunately, was not going to happen as the powers that be declared that the Blackbird would never be operated by civilians (excluding NASA).

Through the USAF Museum Heritage Program, USAF bases that

Its forward fuselage heavily coated with preservative material, this Blackbird still wears its old-style national insignia. The last operating SR-71s carried no form of national insignia, just a small serial on the verticals.

This Blackbird's nose shows the ravages of years of desert storage.

requested SR-71s for static display could easily receive one. The same was also true of legitimate civilian aerospace museums that could show they had the ways and means to care for an SR-71 on display. As previously mentioned, the flyable examples at Beale AFB were sent on one-way missions to various locations for permanent display. The stored examples at Palmdale, however, were another story.

Since the A-12s had sat so long, it would have taken a considerable amount of money and effort to prepare the planes for a one-time only ferry flight this plan was immediately voted down since most museums—especially aviation museums—operate on fairly limited budgets. Some thought was given to moving the aircraft intact but the sheer size of the machine would have made this a difficult if not impossible task, although the nearly complete Blackbirds had been trucked by road from Burbank to Palmdale after the basic airplane had been completed. Covered by heavy canvas, the shrouded aircraft made for quite a

sight as the large vehicle carrying the plane slowly made its way over the mountains to Palmdale for final finishing.

Ben Nattrass, president of Worldwide Aircraft Recovery Systems, had an idea. Nattrass's firm is based in Rockford, Illinois, and has been responsible for the transportation of over 700 aircraft from just about every imaginable locale. Around eight years ago, Nattrass helped a friend ship four disassembled T-28 Trojans from Chino Airport. By using meat trucks, Nattrass managed to get the four planes packed in tight and a new career was begun. The company is the only

one of its type performing such a service and Nattrass has traveled to such remote locations as the Dominican Republic, Honduras, and Alaska to transport aircraft. "Either we are in the middle of the desert or in the Everglades or in Alaska during the middle of winter," commented Nattrass.

Sometimes the aircraft moving business takes strange turns. A couple of years ago, Nattrass moved an F-86 Sabre from Argentina to the US Air Force Academy in Colorado. "It was more for diplomacy than anything else. There were a lot of dinners where swords were exchanged. It was a few years after the Falklands War and it

Once a closely guarded secret, the pilot and RSO cockpits are lit by the desert sun. While in storage, various parts of the aircraft had been scavenged for the operational fleet.

The entire forward fuselage of a Blackbird is seen loaded aboard its transportation trailer. The fuselage of each aircraft was disassembled into two sections.

was a way for the USAF to get back into Argentina," said Nattrass.

One of the company's biggest jobs was moving Kermit Weeks's newly acquired Boeing B-29 Superfortress from Oakland, California. Weeks decided to move the aircraft by land after an attempt to ferry the plane

resulted in losing an engine and having one of the turret covers blow off the plane. The rare B-29 was carefully taken apart and loaded into a fleet of trucks for transportation to Weeks's storage facility.

Worldwide got together with Torrey Engineering and came up with a plan for disassembling the A-12s and SR-71s for transportation to museums. The plan involved breaking each aircraft into five major structural portions. The fuselage was divided into two pieces and the wings were cut into

sections for ease of transportation. The military had already removed many items from each aircraft, and the cutting of the airframe has ensured these aircraft will never again fly. Nattrass employed a crew of six for several months at Palmdale to disassemble and pack four aircraft for shipping to Eglin Air Force Base in Florida, the Alabama Space and Rocket Center in Huntsville, the San Diego Air and Space Museum, and the Pima Air Museum in Tucson, Arizona. The company solicited the SR-71 delivery

The nose section of this Blackbird is marked with its ultimate destination. The Blackbird now on display at Lackland AFB in Texas has, unfortunately, been given a thick coat of ultra-high-gloss black paint. Apparently this was done to protect the machine from the Texas weather but it certainly detracts from the aircraft's unique appearance.

contracts from each of the museums individually.

Plant 42 will also have its own memorial: the SR-71 Blackbird Park.

Plant commander Lt. Col. Scott Allen revealed that a private fund drive was underway to create the park. A retired SR-71 is already in place, and drawings and specifications were undertaken by Carlson Architecture Company. In addition to the SR-71, an A-12 prototype is being renovated to display condition and when parked with the SR-71 will be the first time that the aircraft have been publicly displayed together.

The two aircraft will be placed under a large canopy cover on 2.7 acres of land on one of the airfield's corners

where they will be on display for the public.

For those associated with the Blackbird, it was sad to see the dismembered pieces of the planes sitting on the desert floor as Worldwide went about their business. However, the SR-71 is unusual in that the majority of the fleet is being preserved rather than scrapped. This fact is certainly due to the general public's love and admiration for what is certainly the USAF's best-known aircraft: the Lockheed SR-71 Blackbird.

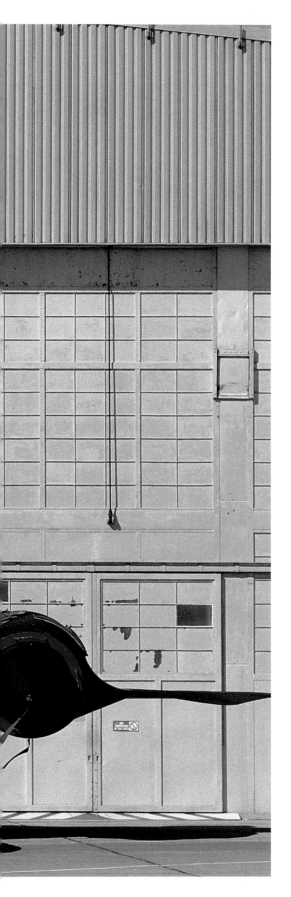

NASA Brings Back the Blackbird

The National Aeronautics and Space Administration (NASA) has always been interested in speed. Indeed, many important developments in advancing the top speed for aircraft have come from NASA's wind tunnels and laboratories and NASA has operated a very wide variety of high-speed aircraft over the years—everything from the North American X-15 rocket ship to the Lockheed YF-12A, predecessor to the SR-71.

NASA obtained the three YF-12As and operated them during the 1970s. These aircraft were outfitted with many different test packages and their flights provided NASA engineers and scientists with lots of data on various regimes of high-speed flight. Assisted by USAF crews, NASA pilots flew a total of 297 flights in two YF-12As and the unique YF-12C. YF-12A s/n 60-6936 was lost on 24 June 1971, after catching fire in flight. Unable to extinguish the fire, the USAF crew ejected from the stricken aircraft. On 7 November 1979, YF-12A s/n 60-6935 made its last flight when the aircraft was flown to Wright-Patterson AFB for permanent exhibition in the USAF Museum.

NASA hopes to use its two SR-71As and one B model in much the same manner as the earlier YF-12s. Currently, the United States is actively involved in the development of the X-30 "space plane." This radical aircraft is designed to takeoff from a conventional runway, fly into a space orbit and then

return to land on another conventional runway. The X-30 has been designed for speeds up to Mach 25 and, needless to say, man-carrying aircraft operating in this speed regime will be subjected to many stresses and forces not previously encountered. New materials and engines will have to be developed to insure the safe operation of such a vehicle.

The Blackbird is an excellent platform for testing equipment and new materials in a moderately high (compared to the X-30) speed range. The ability of the SR-71 to operate in a heat environment of 500 to 1,000 degrees Farenheit can be done more efficiently than using a test unit on the ground. Since the materials going into the X-30 will require extensive testing, it looks like the SR-71 will be the ideal vehicle.

At the time of our February 1991 visit to NASA's Dryden Research Facility at Edwards AFB, NASA crews chosen for Blackbird operations were undergoing some heavy-duty training. NASA has scheduled Rogers Smith and Steve Ishmael to do the piloting honors while the flight test engineers will be Bob Meyer and Marta Bohn-Meyer. This husband and wife team are both pilots and enjoy competition aerobatics in their Pitts Special biplane. Marta will become the first female SR-71 crewmember, although at least one woman has flown in a USAF SR-71B.

At the time of the USAF cancellation of the Blackbird program, the surviving SR-71B was undergoing deep overhaul at Palmdale. Fortunately, the overhaul was completed and the SR-71B will probably be making the first Blackbird flight in NASA colors when the plane is flown from Palmdale to the NASA facility—

Lockheed SR-71A 17980 in front of one of the NASA Dryden hangars—a facility which has seen more than its share of unusual aircraft over the years. Three Blackbirds have been transferred to NASA.

Ishmael and Marta Bohn-Meyer will operate as one of NASA's pilot/engineer teams. Bohn-Meyer is also in charge of accumulating Blackbird assets for the NASA program and has done a great deal to insure that large supplies of spares are safely in hand.

Rogers Smith (in the cockpit) and Steve Ishmael will be the pilots initially operating NASA's Blackbirds as the aircraft explore the regimes of high-speed/high-temperature flight.

119

Bob Meyer, Steve Ishmael, Marta Bohn-Meyer, and Rogers Smith pose with "their" Blackbird. The four will comprise NASA's initial SR-71 flight crew.

Smith and Ishmael wear their Dave Clark suits in front of 17980 which still wears its dart board insignia seen elsewhere in this book.

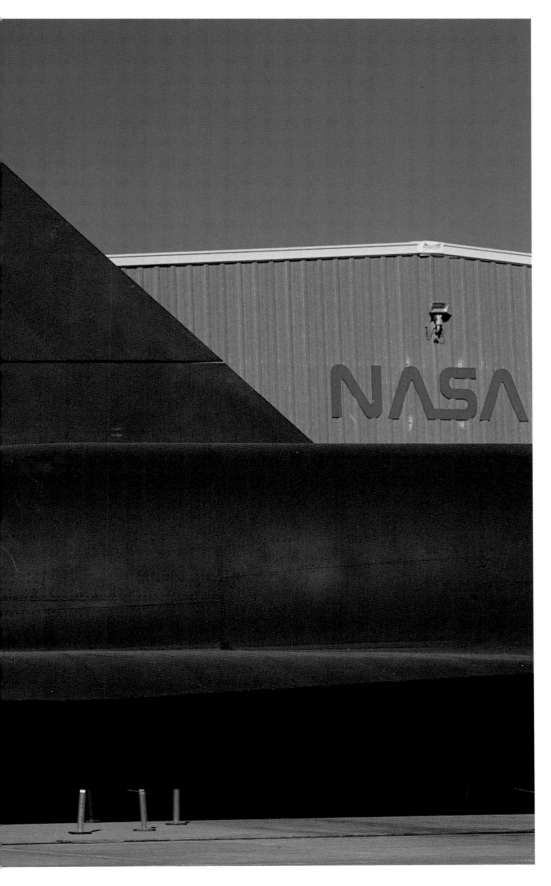

an event scheduled for June or July of 1991.

NASA and the USAF have gone to great efforts to make sure that the Blackbird trio will be well-supplied with vital components. An ample supply of J58 engines and important airframe components has been set aside from the aircraft being dismantled for museum display. Since NASA knew that the USAF would retire the Blackbird fleet within a certain time period, they made plans to obtain the unique SR-71 simulator.

The simulator is a vital component for the operation of the SR-71. About two years ago, NASA personnel went to the Singer-Link facility in New York where the simulator was receiving a $22 million rebuild and modernization. USAF pilots had a chance to give some of the NASA people a run-through on the system and the unit was carefully dismantled after the rebuild was completed and shipped to the Dryden Flight Research Facility, arriving in the summer of 1990.

Crews that have "flown" the simulator state that the effect of flying is quite remarkable—especially when the programmers hand the crews multiple emergencies when flying at Mach 3 and 80,000 feet. The entire simulator was upgraded to a high degree and the instructor's panel controls new software and computers that allow for many new procedural scenarios. The instructor also now has more flexibility in controlling the crew members together or individually.

Steve Ishmael, who had some NASA YF-12 experience, has been given the responsibility of coming up with a plan for checking out NASA's Blackbird crews. Fortunately, support for the SR is high among many previous Blackbird officers still serving with the USAF and he has managed to call upon the expertise of these individuals while obtaining additional valuable input from people retired from the Blackbird program. Time is an important factor to Ishmael since he realizes the longer the Blackbirds sit, the harder they will be to maintain in airworthy condition.

NASA's newly-installed logo on Blackbird 17971, one of the two A models obtained by the organization.

Marta Bohn-Meyer and a NASA engineer monitor the functions of the recently rebuilt and upgraded SR-71 simulator—the only one of its type in existence.

Also, with the passage of time, the talent pool becomes more spread out as people retire or transfer to new positions.

As of May 1991, a final decision had not been made on the problem of aerial refueling. Aerial refueling was an absolute must when the Blackbird was operational but, with the less demanding NASA requirements, NASA SRs may takeoff with a heavy fuel load and accelerate immediately to altitude rather than the USAF routine of taking off light and going immediately to a tanker.

The first-ever uncensored photograph of the SR-71A's pilot's cockpit. Although a product of technology from the 1950s and 1960s, the layout is efficient and easy to scan.

In the simulator, Bob Meyer and Marta Bohn-Meyer are well on their way to achieving about 150 hours of sim time before they make their actual first

Marta Bohn-Meyer in the "second seat" of the Blackbird simulator.

flights in the Blackbird. Both have received high marks from their instructors for the quick grasp of the systems—both are aeronautical engineers. Bohn-Meyer has also been tasked with the formidable job of

managing all of NASA's SR-71 assets so she has been busy checking out USAF depots for hard-to-find items essential for the Blackbird's operation. She has accumulated astro-inertial navigation systems, engines and related components, computers, and even the start carts fitted with two hot rod Buick engines! Some of the items are rather "vintage" and difficult to find.

NASA has developed a talented flight and maintenance crew for operating their trio of Blackbirds and has also received pledges of assistance from many former flight and ground crewmembers—all at no charge—who want to keep the greatest of all USAF aircraft in the air—where the Blackbird belongs!